my teen has had sex

now what do I do?

my teen has had sex

now what do I do?

---

how to help teens make

safe, sensible, self-reliant choices

when they've already said "yes"

---

maureen lyon, ph.d.
and christina breda antoniades

FAIR WINDS
PRESS
BEVERLY, MASSACHUSETTS

Text © 2009 Maureen Lyon, Ph.D., and Christina Breda Antoniades

First published in the USA in 2009 by
Fair Winds Press, a member of
Quayside Publishing Group
100 Cummings Center
Suite 406-L
Beverly, MA 01915-6101
www.fairwindspress.com

13 12 11 10 09   1 2 3 4 5

ISBN-13: 978-1-59233-359-2
ISBN-10: 1-59233-359-1

Library of Congress Cataloging-in-Publication Data
Lyon, Maureen E.
      My teen has had sex : now what do I do? : how to help teens
make safe, sensible, self-reliant choices when they've already said
yes / Maureen Lyon and Christina Breda Antoniades.
            p. cm.
      Includes bibliographical references.
      ISBN-13: 978-1-59233-359-2
      ISBN-10: 1-59233-359-1
   1. Sex instruction for teenagers.   2. Parent and teenager.
I. Antoniades, Christina Breda.   II. Title.
HQ35. L96   2009
649'. 65—dc22
                                                    2008032971

Cover and book design Kathie Alexander

Printed and bound in USA

*The information in this book is for educational purposes only.
It is not intended to replace the advice of a physician or medical
practitioner. Please see your health care provider before beginning
any new health program.*

Contents

About This Book

If you're reading this book, we congratulate you. Whether you just found out your teen is sexually active, or you suspect she is (or soon will be), picking up this book is a good step to guiding your teen through the years ahead.

You may be a little shell-shocked, especially if you've just discovered your teen is no longer a virgin. You're not alone. Even the most open-minded parents have some degree of fear as a child takes those big steps into adulthood. Compounding the worry is the fact that American culture has long portrayed sex before marriage as everything from slightly risqué to taboo to outright dangerous, while at the same time, casual, frequent, and expected.

Our philosophy is that sex is a normal, natural part of human relationships, even for teens—provided it's in the context of a healthy relationship, in which both parties are equally respected, have equal expectations, and are supportive and mindful of each others' feelings.

We also believe that teens should be treated with respect and dignity, and that by providing them with medically accurate information and engaging them in thoughtful discussion, parents can help them grow into adults who make smart, safe, and savvy decisions about sex.

But just how do we define smart, safe, and savvy when it comes to sexual decision making? There's no one answer. For one person in one situation, it may mean abstaining from sexual intercourse. For another person in a different situation, it might mean something else entirely. Generally speaking, though, "smart, safe, and savvy" means teens are taking measures to protect their health, as well as their physical and emotional well-being.

OUR APPROACH

It's natural for parents to worry, regardless of whether their teen is a boy or a girl. We recognize that while mothers of daughters may be the most likely readers of this book, mothers and fathers alike worry about their teens of both sexes. Teenage boys, although often portrayed as eternally sex-driven and emotionally detached, face many of the same challenges as teenage girls when it comes to sexual relationships—like girls, they're at risk for sexually transmitted infections, they can be deeply affected by a teen pregnancy, and they can be emotionally harmed when an intimate relationship ends or doesn't meet their expectations. Therefore, we'll address issues that affect both sexes, and throughout this book when we talk about teens we'll alternate genders, referring to boys in some examples and girls in others. We'll also direct our advice to parents, although we recognize that caregivers, teachers, and other adults may be reading as well.

In addition, we assume that some subset of teens will be gay, lesbian, bisexual, transgender, or questioning (GLBTQ). In many cases, the guidance for parents of GLBTQ teens will closely mirror that of their straight-teen counterparts. But there will be some differences, and we'll address those in sidebars throughout the book. We also recommend that you seek out additional resources on GLBTQ teens and have included some in the resources section of this book.

We also assume there is a relatively healthy relationship between parent and teen. If your teen is strongly confrontational or troubled, you may need further guidance in the form of family counseling or books tailored to the needs of such teens and their parents. We also know that for some parents, our values-neutral approach will be impossible. If you're having an extremely hard time dealing with your teen's sexuality—or talking to your teen in a way that is productive—don't beat yourself up. But do seek out counseling for yourself so that you can come to terms with the reality, and put your teen in touch with someone who can provide information and resources on safer sex and healthy relationships.

Finally, throughout the book, we'll refer to sex and sexual activity. As you'll see in chapter 3, defining those terms can be an exercise in creativity. Teens today have their own ideas about what constitutes sex, and you likely do as well. In this book, however, we'll define sex as vaginal or anal intercourse, and sexual activity as any activity between two people in which the genitals of at least one of the people is stimulated.

You'll also notice that we use the term *sexually transmitted infection (STI)* in place of the more familiar *sexually transmitted disease (STD)*, as is increasingly the practice among health professionals. The reason: the term *disease* implies there are visible or noticeable symptoms, while *infection* merely refers to the presence of a pathogen. Since STIs often occur without symptoms—or produce symptoms that go unnoticed—we'll go with the broader term. Of course, if you're more comfortable saying STD when talking to your teen, you can certainly do so.

OUR TOOLS

Life isn't scripted. We can't hand you your lines, push you onto the stage (where your teen has also miraculously agreed to perform), and expect you to bow thirty minutes later to the sound of applause.

That's because the course of every conversation depends on the personalities of the people involved, their mood at that moment, the particulars of the situation, their relationship with each other, and other factors. So we haven't come up with a one-size-fits-all script to guide you through conversations about sex and sexuality. But we have included sample conversations in the boxes titled, "One Way to Say It ..." Think of them as just that: one way to say it. Then tailor them to fit your teen.

You can find help in focusing the conversation to fit your teen's age by using the "Teen Targeted" sections in the book. These sections offer advice based on the age of your teen (we've broken them out as under fifteen, fifteen to seventeen, and eighteen and over). Use them as general guidelines—teens vary in maturity, and therefore your teen may not fall neatly into his age group—and tweak them accordingly.

We've also included several "Ask the Expert" question-and-answer sections. Again, they may not address your situation exactly, but we're hopeful that they will offer insight you can use.

We've talked to teens, parents, medical professionals, and youth advocates—and used the clinical experience of Dr. Lyon's eighteen years in practice—in an attempt to address the challenges (and opportunities) you're likely to encounter as you guide your teen. Some of our advice will apply to you, and some will not. If you have a particular concern, you might find yourself flipping ahead to get quick advice. That's a natural inclination, but do be sure to go back later and read the book from start to finish. Once you begin the journey of guiding your sexually active teen, you'll no doubt encounter issues and questions you hadn't given thought to before.

You can also visit our website at www.myteenhashadsex.com for more information or to contact the authors. In the meantime, we hope you enjoy the book and find it useful in helping you help your teen.

Sincerely,

Maureen Lyon, Ph.D.
Christina Breda Antoniades

The Limitations of Research

Throughout this book we'll refer to research on behaviors and perceptions. Such studies tell us a lot about how people think, behave, and respond, and can offer a reality check for parents—clueing them in to a world they may not know enough about. That can be useful in helping you determine what your teen might be thinking or doing and how you can help. But keep in mind that research speaks to the behavior of a large group of people. Your teen may or may not fall within the average range. Use the research presented in this book as a general guideline, but be sure to also consider all the additional information you have about your own teen.

CHAPTER 1

Getting a Grip:
How to Cope with the New Reality ...
and Your Own Feelings

Okay, you just found out your teen is having sex. Maybe you discovered a condom in the trash can or stumbled upon a risqué text message that left little room for doubt. Or maybe your teenage daughter has come to you asking for birth control after a pregnancy scare. Suddenly, like it or not, you're faced with the fact that your teen is sexually active.

Your first instinct may be to buy a heavy-duty lock and confine your teen to her room until she's thirty or start a screamfest that ends in you demanding that your son hit the books and steer clear of the girlfriend you'd rather he didn't have. Inwardly, you might lament your child's passage into this new life stage and wish you could keep your teen in the cocoon of childhood for a little bit longer.

You may feel angry, sad, scared, or even guilty over such a discovery. On the other hand, you may feel it's natural and greet the news with acceptance, seeing your teen's move to sexuality as a natural step on the path to adulthood.

Whether you view it as another parenting challenge, a full-blown crisis, or something in between depends on a variety of factors, including your teen's age and maturity level, your own value system, your experience as an adolescent, and even how you discovered the news.

Whatever your emotions, this latest development will likely kick your parental engine into overdrive as you help your teen navigate the emotional and physical trials of sexual relationships. The goal is to help your teen become a savvy, sensible, and responsible adult who makes informed decisions about sex and the relationships to come.

The first step is getting a grip on your own emotions, which means you'll have to consider how you feel, think about why you feel that way, assess your value system, and finally, come to terms with reality.

SO, HOW *DO* YOU FEEL?

Your teen may be sixteen and sexually mature, but this is your baby we're talking about, so it's not unthinkable that you'll have an emotional reaction to the news. Before you take any action, it's a good idea to explore your own emotions.

First, understand that there's no right or wrong way to feel. Your reaction will depend greatly on your circumstances. A mother of a sixteen-year-old boy will likely react differently than a mother of a sixteen-year old girl. A highly impulsive teen—who has a history of leaping first and looking second—will raise more red flags than a teen who has displayed greater maturity and reasoned thinking. Having the news gently broken to you by a family friend will likely elicit a different response than would catching your teenage daughter in bed with her boyfriend.

Perhaps the biggest determining factor is your own value system and your experience as a teen. For a parent who had no inhibitions as an adolescent, it may come as no surprise that a teen is sexually active. This parent may view the teen's decision as perfectly natural and even expected. As such, there may be little problem accepting the reality or focusing on how to help a teen make smart decisions regarding sex. On the other hand, the uninhibited teen can also grow into a highly concerned parent if he or she feels regret about having been sexually active as a teenager.

For parents whose background is socially conservative or strongly religious, the news may be extremely disturbing. The parents may feel that their teen is violating a moral or religious code or treading prematurely in adult waters. Under those circumstances, the parent may feel angry, ashamed, or fearful for the teen's physical, emotional, and spiritual well-being.

There are lots of possibilities in between. Consider your own feelings. Are you:

- angry?
- sad?
- shocked?
- disappointed?
- fearful for your teen's well-being (physical, emotional, or spiritual)?
- guilty?
- relieved?
- feeling another emotion? (If so, what is it?)

Dig Deeper

Once you understand *how* you feel, it's helpful to think about *why* you feel that way. When you understand the cause, you can put your emotions in perspective and work toward coming to terms with them. And when you talk to your teen, you'll be able to better explain why you feel the way you do.

Ask Yourself: Why Do I Feel that Way?

- Do my teen's actions violate my religious or moral beliefs?
- Did I have an early experience with sex that hurt me emotionally, and now I worry that my teen might experience something similar?
- Am I worried about teen pregnancy or sexually transmitted infections?
- Do I see my teen's sexuality as a sign that he hasn't adopted my value system?
- Do I see my teen's actions as evidence that I'm a bad parent?
- Am I angry about being deceived by my teen?
- Am I worried about what other family members will say?
- Am I worried my teen will get a bad reputation in the community?
- Am I upset about the type of activity my teen is engaged in?

- Do I feel disappointed that my teen didn't have the experience I'd envisioned for her?
- Am I uncomfortable with the thought of my child growing up because it makes me feel old?

How your answers influence your response will depend on your situation. Suppose, for example, that you explore your emotions, and find that what you thought was anger is really fear. Perhaps your own college plans were derailed when you got pregnant, and you fear the same for your teen. Understanding this might lead you less to demanding that your teen refrain from sex, and more toward educating her about pregnancy prevention. On the other hand, if a deeper look at your emotions reveals a fear that you've failed as a parent, you may have some internal work to do: exploring what kind of parent you really are and educating yourself about the realities of teens and sex.

Uncomfortable, but Not Unreasonable, Feelings

For some parents, confronting an adolescent's sexuality triggers emotional struggles that have more to do with the parent's experience than the teen's.

Odd as it may seem, it's not unusual for parents to feel jealous of a teen's sexuality. After all, parents of teens typically are entering midlife—which may also be a time when sex lives or romantic relationships are slumping—while their teens are growing into a time of promise and potential. A teen's sexuality may spark feelings of yearning for the days when the parent was young and experiencing sex for the first time, or free to experiment sexually, or for a renewed interest in her own sexual desires. Some parents will feel disturbed by feelings of jealousy, but such feelings shouldn't be viewed as unhealthy. They're quite normal and reasonable.

Sometimes parents also experience a sense of powerlessness or abandonment as a teen's affection and attention turns toward a third party. This, too, is normal.

Parents who were sexually molested or assaulted in the past may find that dealing with their own child's sexuality brings up feelings or unresolved issues and may even trigger anxiety or depression. Some abuse or assault victims may find it necessary to seek out counseling to deal with those feelings.

For a detailed look at parental responses to a child's adolescence, check out *Crossing Paths: How Your Child's Adolescence Triggers Your Own Crisis*, by Laurence Steinberg with Wendy Steinberg.

ASSESS YOUR VALUES

Conflict surrounding a teen's sexuality usually arises when the behavior violates a parent's values. If you have strong feelings on the subject of sexuality, chances are you've indirectly given your child indicators all along, perhaps through involvement with a religious group, by the movies you allow your teen to see, or the type of music you object to. Ideally, you've also had discussions with your teen over the years about your family's values and how you view sex and sexuality. Such discussions, started early in life, are important given that teens are bombarded with sexualized messages from the media and may have other influences—such as widely available pornography—shaping their views of themselves and the world (we'll go into this in greater depth in chapter 3).

If you haven't thought through or talked about your family values or beliefs, now is the time to get started. Think about what you believe. Even if your teen has already determined she doesn't share the same value system (and that's not a given, by the way) you'll be better able to explain your feelings if you can articulate your own beliefs.

Ask Yourself: Do I Object To
- sex outside of marriage?
- sex outside of a committed relationship?
- sex for teens under a certain age or maturity level?

Are My Objections Based On
- religion? If not, what is the basis?
- sex with a particular partner?
- certain types of sexual behavior?

Are There Behaviors I Simply Cannot Accept?
- If so, what are they?

Respect Your Teen's Values
Bear in mind that your teen is still developing his own value system, and it's subject to change without notice. Some teens may view casual sex as no big deal now, but with more information and experience, they may come to see it in a different light (or maybe not).

Parents and caregivers can encourage adolescents to develop values by engaging in thoughtful conversations about sex and relationships. This doesn't mean forcing a teen to adopt your own values, although they may be the values you hope your teen will embrace. Teens have to determine for themselves what they believe is "wrong" and then give up or avoid those behaviors, or what is "right" and follow through in a responsible way.

If you have strong religious convictions that conflict with your teen's values, it may not be easy to respect his right to his own value system. Talking to your priest, minister, rabbi, or other spiritual leader might offer you some insight and consolation. Bringing your teen into the conversation might also be helpful, but only if you're sure it will be a thoughtful, open discussion rather than a lecture or browbeating.

ASSESS THE REALITIES

So, your teenager has had sex. Is it possible to convince her not to do it again? Or should you accept the reality and forget about trying to sway your teen? The answer, not surprisingly, is "it depends."

Generally, we don't advise a goal of getting a teen to "stop," as in, "forever" or even "for the next five years." We do, however, advocate an effort aimed at getting teens to stop long enough to think before they act. This is especially true for teens who have become sexually active impulsively, without having given the decision much thought. By talking to your teen about the experience, you'll help bring about personal conclusions on whether being sexually active is the right thing, right now.

Some teens will decide without much prodding that they're not really ready to be sexually active and will wait before they experiment again. Others will decide after a calm, thoughtful discussion to hold off on more sexual activity for any number of reasons (we've even heard some teens say they're too busy or too focused on school to maintain a sexual relationship). Still others will decide that their decision is right for them and will continue to be sexually active, with or without their parents' understanding. But even for those teens, "stopping to think" can help make sure they act responsibly each and every time they have sex.

Educate Yourself

Understanding the realities of teens and sex will help you put your own teen's activities in perspective. You can do that by reading chapter 3, but for a preview, consider the following:

- In the United States, the average age for first sexual intercourse is 16.9 for boys and 17.4 for girls (although some experts caution that exact estimates are impossible to make with any degree of certainty).
- Forty-eight percent of high schoolers report they have had sexual intercourse at least once.[1] The percentage is higher for an older teen (more than 60 percent of high school seniors) and lower for a younger teen (33 percent of ninth graders).
- Having sex once doesn't mean teens are sexually active at any given time. Of the teens who said they'd had sex, only 35 percent said they were currently sexually active, meaning that they had had sex within the past three months.
- Although the percentage of teens who have had sex dropped steadily between 1991 and 2001, the decline has leveled off in recent years (experts are still exploring why that may be).
- Fifteen percent of high schoolers have had four or more sex partners in their lifetime.
- Fifty-five percent of male teens and 54 percent of female teens say they've had oral sex with someone of the opposite sex.

CONSIDER CONTEXT

Whether you'll make an impact on your teen's sexual decisions depends on what's going on in her life. If your seventeen-year-old daughter has been in an exclusive relationship for a year and has decided to have sex with her boyfriend, you may be fighting a losing battle. A sixteen-year-old who reports one random hookup, on the other hand, might decide with your help that he's not ready for more.

The relationship between parent and teen is another consideration. If you haven't had open, honest, and respectful communication about sex in the past, it's unreasonable to expect that you'll sit down with your teen and glide through this particular topic. Your teen might welcome you (and the conversation) with open arms, but might also be uncomfortable or wary of the sudden switch. Be patient, explain your reason for not talking in the past, and use the communication tips outlined in this book.

If you can convince your teen that you're focused on a respectful discussion with safety and well-being in mind, you can probably make up for lost time. If not, you may need to enlist outside help, either in the form of counseling or through a medical professional such as an adolescent medicine doctor (see Finding a Doctor on page 106 and our list of resources at the back of this book).

Teen Targeted: Age Appropriate Response?

Under 15: If your teen is under fourteen and you're upset she's had sex, your instincts are on target. Almost all experts agree that children under fourteen are not mature enough to be in sexual relationships. For fourteen-year-olds, your concerns may still be well founded, since most teens at this age will find sexual relationships to be especially challenging given their maturity level. Keep in mind that even if you're right and your teen's not ready, you still have a limited ability to control what she does with her body. When evaluating your emotions, focus on what it is about your teen's situation that worries you most. It may be that you fear your teen doesn't have enough experience and information to make good decisions about sex, is emotionally unready to handle the intensity of a sexual relationship, or something else entirely. Being aware of specific concerns will help you articulate them for your teen later, when you're ready to talk.

You should also consider the context of the sexual activity. A one-off sexual "experiment" might be less cause for concern than a pattern of behavior, just as random sexual encounters may worry you more than sex within the context of a relationship. Finally, consider the shock factor. If the news hits you as a complete surprise, you may respond more emotionally than if you'd expected it. Understanding that may help you strip away some amplified emotion and focus on the actual issues.

15 to 17: With a teen at the younger end of this age group, you might still be dealing with surprise and shock. But you should be aware that by seventeen, teens are more likely to have had sex than to not have had sex (see chapter 3 for more sexual norms). If you're feeling angry, upset, or otherwise unhappy with the news, do consider the root of your emotions and then work to make sure that your fears aren't realized. Educate your teen about STIs and pregnancy, and make sure she's thinking clearly about her emotional well-being.

18 and over: If you feel your teen is still too young to handle being sexually active, you may be right. But for most teens this age, sex is a natural next step, and yours can probably tackle the ups and downs in much the same way an adult would (and in most senses of the word, your teen *is* an adult). If you're having a strong, emotional reaction, it's important to think about why that might be. Your answer may have more to do with you than with your teen, in which case it may be something you need to work out in your own mind. If you're working on coming to terms with the new reality, it's okay to admit that to your teen, who will probably be glad to hear it.

Cathy's Story

Cathy, a high school senior, was raised in a religious family. After six months of dating her boyfriend, Thomas, she felt she was in love. They hadn't had intercourse but were venturing beyond kissing. Cathy, who'd always gotten the impression from her mother that sex was dirty and unpleasant, was surprised and angry to discover she had strong sexual feelings—and that they were pleasurable. Maybe sex wasn't so bad after all. "They lied to me," she thought. "This isn't wrong or something I need to give up."

Her behavior clearly conflicted with the values she had been raised with—that sex was only to be experienced after marriage, for the purpose of procreation. She felt conflicted between her internal sense of what was right and wrong and what she had been taught.

Cathy decided first to confess to a priest, who told her to stop. "It's only puppy love," he said, "and what you're doing is morally wrong." That left Cathy feeling disrespected and more distant from her religion. Nevertheless, she persisted within the parameters of her faith and sought guidance from her religion teacher, a priest she trusted. Face to face and without judgment, he asked her the following questions: Did her boyfriend treat her well? Did she trust him? Was there privacy? Had she considered the risk of pregnancy? Had she thought ahead to how she might feel if this relationship ended?

As she talked, the picture became clearer in her own mind. She was starting to feel more certain that intercourse outside of marriage wasn't necessarily morally wrong. But she was worried about taking the relationship to a new level of intensity. Thomas was about to join the military. Wouldn't having sex make their separation more painful? And what if she got pregnant? She and Thomas had mutual friends who'd gotten married as a result of an unexpected pregnancy. Thomas had already said he wasn't ready for marriage—and frankly, neither was she. So what *would* she do if she got pregnant?

Cathy's religion teacher never told her what to do. But talking to him helped her clarify her own views. She felt grateful that he treated her with respect and her yearning for sexual intimacy and love as normal.

Cathy decided on her own to stop short of intercourse. Eventually, Thomas joined the military and was stationed overseas. Three months later, Cathy ended the relationship after meeting the young man she would eventually marry.

WORK ON ACCEPTANCE

The older your teen is, the more likely you'll have to accept his independence or risk alienating him entirely. True, you still have influence, but you're moving into a stage of life where negotiation is the norm; you'll no longer be able to issue orders and expect them to be obeyed.

Still, it's important to use your influence and guide your teen into making informed decisions, to help her develop values, and to be there for support. Parenting sexually active teens often comes down to giving them enough room to make those decisions while providing the boundaries and resources a teen needs to stay safe. As with any aspect of parenting a teen, we recommend that you adhere to three basic principles: Respect your teen's independence, be fair, and be honest.

This doesn't mean you need to change your own value system. Rather, you may have to accept the fact that your teen's values differ, and that he or she has a right to those values. If

your values clash, you may have to restate your own beliefs—
"I think it's a mistake to have sex at your age"—while ultimately
supporting your teen's decision—"I want you to be safe, so
I'm here to talk about it if you need me."

Of course, there are times when independence isn't in order.
We'll address this more in chapter 8, but in general, the need to
protect teens takes priority over their independence if the teen is:

- under fourteen
- in an abusive or destructive relationship
- having sex with someone who is more than four years older
  (or more than three years older for teens under sixteen)
- engaging in high-risk sexual activity
- engaging in sexual activity while under the influence of
  alcohol or drugs

In addition, you should be aware that children who were sexually abused in their younger years often face greater challenges
when they reach adolescence and may require counseling as
they move into sexual maturity.

SHARE, BUT WITH CARE

Thinking through your own emotions and value system is important, but at some point it's normal to want to talk to someone
about what you're feeling. Whether it's your teen's other parent,
a family friend, or another adult, having a shoulder to cry on or
a sympathetic ear can be a critical form of emotional support.

For some parents, finding a friend who isn't close to the
teen, and can be trusted to keep mum is a good choice. You
can also find support through religious groups, parenting groups,
a family counselor, or a family doctor, pediatrician, or adolescent
medicine doctor.

There are potentially thorny issues, however. You have an
obligation to protect your teen's privacy and a compelling reason
not to violate his trust. It's fairly common for teenage girls, for
example, to beg Mom not to tell Dad that his baby girl is sexually

active or for a son to swear Dad to secrecy. Whether you agree to such a request depends on your family history—your relationship with your teen's other parent as well as his relationship with the teen—and whether you think the benefit of telling outweighs the risk of violating your teen's trust.

Generally speaking, couples share similar core values. Often, it's what helped bring them together. But that doesn't mean that you and your teen's other parent will react the same way to your child's sexuality. One parent may be more protective of a teen or may have stronger moral objections to a particular situation.

If you and your teen's other parent don't see eye to eye on parenting your sexually active teen, you might try to work it out on your own or seek outside help. Either way, the key is resolving your own conflict so that it doesn't spill over into your interaction with your teen or prevent you from addressing her needs. Couples counseling or parenting classes can help parents work through their issues.

GET A GRIP

If you've ever lost it emotionally, you already know that getting a grip on your feelings is beneficial for you. Or, more accurately, it is significantly less painful than dealing with the fallout that can result from a wildly emotional response.

But there's more to getting a grip than just what it does for you. In fact, understanding and controlling your emotions is incredibly important if you want to have a talk that is respectful, reasoned, and effective. That, in turn, gives you the best possible chance of influencing your teen's behavior and helping him become a healthy, happy, responsible adult.

Consider two real-world examples:

Needs to Get a Grip

A teacher caught fifteen-year-old Sara and a male schoolmate engaging in oral sex on school property. The school principal called her parents, whose immediate reaction was explosive. Sara's mother tearfully berated her, while her father lost control and slapped her.

Sara met her parents' anger with defiance. When she first came in for counseling she was defensive, proclaiming it her right to do with her body whatever she chose. In a safe and nonjudgmental counseling environment, however, Sara had the opportunity she needed to explore her feelings without anger to cloud the picture. She quickly dropped her guard and admitted the sexual encounter had gotten out of control. It had, in fact, made her feel scared and uncomfortable. To top it all off, she worried she'd get a bad reputation at school. With a little prompting, Sara came to her own conclusion: If she had it to do over, she probably wouldn't. And if a similar situation arose, she'd want to set limits on what happened, where it happened, and with whom.

When counseled, Sara's parents were able to see that their anger stemmed from several places: fear that their daughter was too young to be sexually active, anger that she was engaging in behavior she knew they wouldn't approve of, and embarrassment over the public nature of the activity. In time, Sara and her parents were able to develop a level of trust and talk through issues without angry outbursts. But much of their energy went toward undoing that early damage when it could have been better spent listening to and guiding their teen.

Got a Grip

Lynn knew something was bothering her daughter, Jessica. The sixteen-year-old had been silent throughout dinner, and instead of rushing upstairs to chat online with friends, she'd lingered after the meal. Clearly she wanted to talk. Finally, Jessica dropped a bombshell: She and her boyfriend of nearly a year had been having sex for three months, and Jessica was worried she might be pregnant.

Lynn, a single mother who had encouraged her daughter to wait until she was older to have sex, was shocked and appalled. One look at her daughter's face, however, told her that what Jessica needed at that moment was a little reassurance, and maybe a hug.

Lynn steered Jessica to the living room, where they could sit quietly and talk. She admitted to Jessica that the news upset her, but reassured her daughter that she was there to help.

She praised Jessica for coming to her to talk. Then she asked a few initial questions to address Jessica's immediate concerns. She asked:

- What kind of sexual activity did Jessica engage in?
- Had she used any protection?
- What made her think she might be pregnant?
- How long had it been since she'd menstruated?
- Did she have any other symptoms?

Keeping in mind her daughter's emotional state, Lynn worked hard to sound supportive, reassuring, and nonjudgmental. After hearing her daughter's answers, Lynn suspected Jessica wasn't pregnant. But she suggested they buy a home pregnancy test and follow up with a visit to an adolescent medicine doctor regardless of the results. There Jessica could get more information on pregnancy prevention and get screened for STIs. For now, addressing Jessica's immediate health concerns was paramount.

Later, Lynn would evaluate her own emotions and come to terms with the reality that her daughter was sexually active. She realized that she was afraid for her daughter's emotional state. Lynn had been emotionally manipulated as a sexually active teen and wanted her daughter to avoid the same pain. To that end, she talked more with Jessica, gently asking her how she felt about being sexually active, what she wanted from the relationship, and if she felt that the relationship was an emotionally healthy one.

DON'T GIVE UP

Of course, keeping your cool isn't easy, especially in the heat of the moment. If your teen initiated the conversation, or if your discovery has already led to a confrontation, you may not have had time to think through your reaction. You might even have found yourself reacting badly and fear you've already botched things with your teen.

It's true that an angry or overly emotional reaction can close doors, but in many cases they're not closed for good, which means that even if you've already talked to your teen—and feel you didn't do it well—there's plenty of room to recover. In fact, it might be helpful to view the situation as an opportunity to open or renew a discussion with your teen. Handle it well, and you'll turn a potential crisis into a learning experience that lasts a lifetime.

My Teen Is GLBTQ

Discovering that your teen is sexually active can be upsetting enough, but finding out a child has engaged in same-sex activity can be particularly hard for some parents to accept.

Parents may object to such sexual activity on moral or religious grounds, may be fearful for their teen's emotional or physical safety, or may be dealing with their own disappointment that their teen's behavior falls outside of what society still dictates as "normal." Even adults who are otherwise gay-friendly can have trouble accepting the fact that their teen is gay, lesbian, bisexual, transgender, or questioning (GLBTQ) because it flies in the face of their expectations.

If you've just discovered your teen has had a same-sex encounter, you might still be coming to terms with what that means (if anything). It's helpful to put the discovery into perspective. Keep in mind that the teenage years are a time of experimentation in all aspects of life. Your teen's activities or feelings may or may not be an indicator of future orientation (and remember, too, that teens who do identify as GLBTQ have not necessarily had any sexual activity—same-sex or otherwise).

Although many people say they knew their orientation from very early on in life, not all do. Whatever a teen ultimately determines her orientation or gender identity to be, your teen is still the same person you knew and loved before sexual orientation or identity entered the picture.

Just as you would with a straight teen, you'll need to go through the steps outlined in the previous pages: understanding your own emotions and their root cause, identifying your values, and reconciling them with reality. And remember the three guiding principles: Respect your teen's independence, be fair, and be honest.

UNDERSTAND YOUR EMOTIONS

As you go through this process, think about what's at the root of any negative feelings you may be having. In addition to the questions you'd ask yourself regardless of your teen's orientation or gender identity, you may also want to explore some questions specifically relating to your teen being GLBTQ. They are (this is not an exhaustive list— do think about other issues that may apply to you):

- Am I worried that my teen won't have the future I envisioned, including getting married and having children?
- Am I upset because being GLBTQ violates my religious values?
- Am I worried about STIs?
- Am I worried about what the family (or neighbors, or community at large) will think?
- Am I upset because I think my teen won't be happy?
- Do I feel guilty that my parenting may have "caused" my teen to be gay?
- Am I sad that my teen is going through what may be a difficult realization and adjustment?

- Am I worried my teen will be harassed or bullied?
- Do I feel unprepared to help my teen navigate the teen years when his experience will be so much different from mine?

The concerns that caused your initial negative reaction may prove to be unfounded. Many GLBTQ teens grow into adults who have children and live in long-term committed relationships, including, in some places, marriage or civil unions. And most gay teens will tell you they're happier living their lives honestly—even if that causes conflict—than trying to live a lie, which may put your "unhappy life" fears to rest.

Although society has a long way to go toward creating an inclusive environment for people regardless of orientation or gender identity, acceptance and understanding of GLBTQ people has made great gains, which means your concerns about the social fallout may be overblown. Finally, if your fears stem from guilt, you should know that although science hasn't nailed down a reason why some people are attracted to the same sex or identify with the opposite gender, the "cause" isn't parenting or mental illness.

ASSESS YOUR VALUES

As you go through the process, your questions will be similar to the ones you'd have if your child were straight. Your goal is to clarify for yourself exactly what your values are and, specifically, what behaviors you object to.

Ask yourself: Do I object to
- sex before marriage, regardless of the gender of the people engaging in it?
- any sex between two people of the same gender?

- casual sex?
- risky sex?
- a sexual orientation or gender identity that is different from the majority?

If you have strong moral or religious objections to same-sex relationships or sexual activity and your teen is GLBTQ, you may have to choose between rigid adherence to your beliefs (at the risk of driving your teen away) and finding a way to accept your teen. (For an excellent discussion of this from someone who's been there, read *Always My Child* by Kevin Jennings.)

Talking to your priest, rabbi, or other spiritual leader may help you find a way to come to terms with your teen's orientation or gender identity. There are also support programs for families of gender variant children, such as the one at Children's National Medical Center in Washington, D.C.

CONSIDER YOUR TEEN'S FEELINGS

So far, you've focused mainly on how your teen's orientation or gender identity (or the questioning of either) feels to you. But don't forget that this is really about your teen, whose feelings and concerns should be paramount. In most cases, GLBTQ youth don't have a parent who has been through what they're going through, much less one who can instill in them a sense of pride in being GLBTQ. That fact just adds to the sense of isolation GLBTQ teens already may feel and makes it even more important for you to focus squarely on your teen's needs. It also highlights the need for parents to help teens create a support network that includes people who can relate to their experience.

If you're straight, think about how challenging it was to come to terms with your own sexuality. Now think about how much more difficult that would be for someone who also has to deal with a social stigma, fear of rejection from family, and even fear of harassment and violence.

Of course, your needs count, too. Most parents of GLBTQ teens can benefit from talking to others who've gone through a similar experience and educating themselves about the rights and realities of GLBTQ youth. The back of this book contains some helpful resources.

CHAPTER 2

Before You Talk:
Understand Your Goals and
Teen Development

If you suspect or have just discovered that your teen is sexually active, you might be struck with an uncontrollable sense of urgency. Is she using birth control? Does he know about STIs? Your mind might be screaming, TALK NOW.

And you should talk—and then, talk more. Your teen needs you in ways that he or she never has before. Do it right, and you will play some important roles: a primary resource for reliable information about sex and contraception, a sounding board for your teen's thoughts, and a steady hand guiding him toward smart and healthy decisions regarding sex. Fail to talk, and you miss an opportunity to influence your teen's choices and to take an active part in shaping her into a happy, healthy adult.

So, yes, definitely, talk. But before you do, spend some time identifying exactly what you hope to accomplish.

Ask yourself: Do I hope to
- convince my teen that sex outside of marriage is morally wrong?
- convince my teen that sex is dangerous and unpleasant (so she'll decide against it)?
- guilt, threaten, or cajole my teen into abstaining from sex from now on?

If you answered yes to any of the questions above, you'll do well to rethink your approach. It's neither realistic nor helpful to assume that you can threaten or cajole anyone into abstinence. Your teen may stop out of fear of disappointing you or risking punishment—but it's far more likely that she will simply stop talking about it and continue being sexually active without the benefit of your input. And if your teen feels disrespected or lied to, it's likely to damage your relationship in the long run.

YOUR GOAL: OPEN COMMUNICATION

We know from research that when there is good communication between teens and mothers, for example, teens are more likely to practice abstinence. Such communication rests on an open, nonjudgmental discussion in which each party shows respect for the other. And it should happen over many conversations rather than in one all-encompassing "sex talk." In fact, teens and parents alike consistently report that the "birds and the bees" talk is uncomfortable at best and unhelpful at worst.

Instead, it's best to seize upon "teachable moments," during which you send the message that sex is an adult action with adult consequences, both physical and emotional, and therefore requires responsible behavior.

Although it won't stop teens from having sex, striving for open, ongoing communication has a positive impact on several levels:

- **It strengthens the bond between parents and teens.**
  Adolescents are in the midst of an exciting and challenging transition from childhood to adulthood. They are growing and determining the individuals they will become. By talking and listening to each other, you'll build a trusting and respectful relationship that can offer your teen the support that's needed now and into adulthood.
- **It ensures that teens can get reliable information and medical care.** You cannot let your teen rely on information from friends, the Internet, or school. Some of it is flat-out wrong; other sources simply won't reflect your values. As long as you're in the picture, you can make sure that your teen is

getting good information that presents sex in a way you're comfortable with.

- **It allows parents to encourage sexual responsibility.** An open discussion gives parents the chance to highlight risks, express concerns, and influence their teen's behavior. Parents can offer guidance in setting limits on sexual activity so that teens are less likely to make choices they'll later regret. They can role-play how to say no and how to negotiate condom use.

- **It helps teens view their parents as a resource.** When parents open the door, teens have a far easier time coming to them as a resource if a crisis strikes. That crisis may be big, small, or somewhere in between—life-altering or merely life-shaping.

- **It helps parents develop in their teenagers a healthy view of sex.** Sexuality can be a tremendously satisfying part of human relationships. But teens, especially GLBTQ teens, often are given the message—sometimes by well-meaning adults—that sex is dangerous, scary, or harmful. By talking about sex, you remove the taboo and help your teen grow into a sexually healthy, happy, loving adult.

Opening Up Isn't Always Easy

As with most solutions, there are some downsides. The most obvious one is that such an approach requires you to let go of what is, for many people, a natural inclination to make decisions for their child of any age. This can be especially hard if you don't share the same values.

And let's face it, talking about sex can be uncomfortable, for you and your teen. You probably don't want to talk or think about your teen having sex any more than your teen wants to think about you having sex (trust us). But the more you make talking a natural part of your relationship, the more comfortable you'll feel. It's good to remember, especially in those squeamish moments, that the long-term benefits of talking to your teen about sex are much more important and lasting than the temporary discomfort you may feel.

Lynn's Story

Lynn, a nineteen-year-old freshman in college, had been dating Nick for more than a year. Phoning home, she asked her parents (who were both on the line) if she and Nick could use the family's summer cottage for the weekend.

Her parents, Rita and Larry, were shocked and upset. Both quickly said no and angrily reminded her about their values: They don't approve of sex outside of marriage.

Lynn was angry that her parents assumed she was having sex. Her mother snapped back, "Well, are you?" Lynn, on the defensive, tersely told her mother that she and Nick were not, in fact, having sex, but that she had had sex for the first time in the *tenth* grade. Again, Rita and Larry were shocked and upset at hearing the news so abruptly on the phone.

Lynn said she'd wanted to talk to her mother about her first sexual relationship when it happened, especially since she was devastated when it ended, but she hadn't been able to. She complained that the family never talked about sex and so she hadn't felt she *could* talk about it.

Rita realized she'd missed an opportunity to help her daughter through an emotional time. The call ended with a teary goodbye and all three promising to talk more. Larry remained angry that Lynn had had sex at such a young age. Rita was more upset than angry; she confided to a friend that she felt shocked by the revelation and that she ached at the thought of Lynn going through such turmoil alone.

When Lynn visited home the next weekend, Rita set aside time for the two to talk. She knew Larry was still too emotional, so she suggested he sit out this conversation. Lynn and Rita then sat down and talked about Lynn's first relationship, how she felt about her current boyfriend, and what she needed to think about when deciding whether and when to have sex with him. Rita reminded Lynn that if they did have sex, it would make their separations more painful, as her boyfriend attended a college out of state and they would not be able to see each other regularly.

At the end of the conversation, Rita suggested that Lynn make an appointment to see her gynecologist so she could get information on birth control and STI prevention before she had sex again. Lynn had been to the gynecologist before but hadn't felt the need at the time to talk about birth control and STIs. Now, she agreed, would be a good time.

CHANGING BODIES, DEVELOPING BRAINS

As you prepare to move forward in an ongoing discussion with your teen, it's helpful to understand what's going on in his or her body and mind. The term *adolescence* refers to all the physical, social, emotional, and psychological changes a child goes through between the ages of roughly thirteen and nineteen years. It is a transitional period between childhood and adulthood.

And while it's often billed as a tumultuous time, it's important to remember that, stereotypes aside, most teens aren't in major conflict with their parents. They can be confounding at times, but most do reasonably well in school, follow rules, love their parents, and grow into healthy adults.

Still, there's no denying that this time of life can be turbulent, trying, and confusing. You might remember it yourself, those awkward years where you are suddenly forced to cope with a body that is morphing by the minute—sprouting hair, acne, and fleshy bits out of nowhere—while coming to grips with a new social order at home. At home you're struggling to prove to your parents that you're no longer a baby—and maybe feeling the pros and cons of that extra responsibility you'd been begging for. And at school relationships are turned on their head, too, as your focus turns to potential love interests instead of merely friends. All the while you're contending with a host of new emotions and urges. It's an exciting period of possibility but also an alarming time of change.

By the time they reach early adolecence, most teens have developed their own personalities, interests, and preferences. They're changing in ways that affect how they see the world and interact with everyone, from their parents, to teachers, to the girl or boy next door.

No surprise, then, that young teens struggle at times with who they are and how they perceive themselves. They may seem suddenly overly focused on their appearance and feel the dip in self-esteem that goes with wondering how the world views them.

They may also find themselves frustrated as their growing desire to be independent crashes headfirst into the reality that they're still dependent on their parents and others.

Young teens typically have:
- expanded intellectual interests (although for some, this will happen later)
- the capacity to think in the abstract (although for some, this will happen later)
- a greater ability to express themselves
- an increased expectation of independence
- a focus on the present, with less thought given to the future
- an increased interest in sex and worries about being sexually attractive to others
- changes in their social circle as they sort out who they are, along with their likes and dislikes

- concerns about what's normal and whether they fit the mold
- the realization that parents aren't perfect, which may cause them to question your decisions in new ways
- a greater interest in spending more time with friends and less with family

During the early adolescent years they may test boundaries, put a little emotional distance between themselves and their parents, have more conflict with parents, experiment with sex and drugs, and shift from a focus on same-sex friends to a social circle that includes the opposite sex. And although they're more mature than they were, they may still act impulsively and resort to childish behavior at times.

As they grow, teens continue their strides toward independence and often experience a boost in their self-esteem.

Older teens typically have:
- an increased ability to make decisions for themselves
- a firm sense of identity
- the capacity for self-examination
- the ability to think ideas through
- an increased ability to compromise and accept delayed gratification
- increased emotional stability
- increased concern for others
- increased self-reliance
- less focus on peer relationships as other interests gain importance
- less conflict with parents

Older teens also tend to have a greater capacity than younger teens to focus on the future and behave accordingly, solve their own problems, feel confident in their sexual identity, develop serious relationships, and compromise. Although some teens will still struggle with impulsiveness, most will find themselves increasingly less impulsive as they reach their late teens.

The Adolescent Body

All of this is set against the backdrop of puberty, a stage of sexual and physical maturation that lasts about five years. Puberty is reached at different times for girls and boys and can vary widely by individual.

Over the years, the age at which people reach puberty has fallen. Today, girls typically reach puberty between ages eight and seventeen (on average, African American girls hit puberty sooner than the overall population, as do girls who are overweight. Puberty may occur later in girls who exercise a lot).

During puberty, the body releases hormones that trigger changes. For girls, these include a growth spurt, especially in height; breast growth; the emergence of body hair and pubic hair; changes in the vagina, uterus, and ovaries; menstruation; a widening of the hips and a change in body shape; as well as the emergence of acne, body odor, and skin changes. By age seventeen, a girl's physical growth is usually complete.

For boys, puberty usually hits between the ages of nine and sixteen. A boy will also experience a growth spurt, especially in height. His shoulders will broaden, and his penis, scrotum, and testes will grow. He may experience nighttime ejaculation (also called wet dreams). He will grow facial and pubic hair; may develop acne, body odor, and skin changes; and experience a deepening of his voice. He may go through a "fat phase" at about age eleven and have growth in his breasts, although such growth typically goes away by the end of puberty.

Sounds fun, right? But wait, there's more going on in the person formerly known as your baby.

The Adolescent Brain

You may have already noticed that teens can be irrational. They get swept up in their emotions: love, hate, jealousy, admiration. They have impulses. They sometimes make bad decisions. In short, they're just like adults, right? Well, yes and no, at least when it comes to how they think. Perhaps the biggest difference between adults and teens is that teens lack experience to inform their intuition.

But emerging science is showing us that there are other differences as well. In fact, the teen years are now thought to be a time of great change for the brain. Part of this change is a continuation of earlier development. The limbic system, which controls emotions, perceptions, and the processing of social information, is one of the first parts of the brain to develop, for example. That means teens may experience feelings more intensely and be more aware of their social standing than they were as children.

At the same time, the part of the brain that controls *executive function*—which guides behavior according to goals or plans—hasn't caught up yet, making it harder for teens to make snap decisions and control their impulses. The teenage brain is also undergoing a rewiring and restructuring phase, which may add a level of difficulty to decisionmaking.

Studies also show that the teen brain behaves differently than the adult brain when it comes to pleasure seeking and risk-taking. For teens, large rewards trigger a stronger response than they do for adults. As a result, teens are more likely to go for the big bang rather than being content with small gains, making the teenage years a prime time for risk-taking. It may be no coincidence that risk-taking increases at exactly the time that humans are preparing to find a mate and reproduce, which, back in man's early days, would have required a risk-taking mind-set.[2]

The effects, of course, are greater in some teens than in others. Generally, young children who were able to control their impulses—resisting the temptation of cookies, in one study—did better at controlling their impulses in their teen years as well.

Don't Forget the Hormones

Making it all the more complex, the teenage brain is under the influence of hormones, which surge during puberty. In boys, testosterone can overstimulate the amygdala, home to the fight-or-flight impulse and the control center for fear and aggression. A rush of testosterone can trigger anger, aggression, sexual interest, dominance, and territoriality, which can account for a host of volatile behaviors in teenage boys.[3]

Girls, on the other hand, experience great shifts in progesterone and estrogen throughout puberty. Since those hormones impact mood, their changes in levels can result in dramatic mood swings, among other effects.

A Word about Orientation and Identity

In our society, we tend to assume that people are straight and identify their gender according to the genitals with which they were born.

But advocates for gay, lesbian, bisexual, transgender, and questioning (GLBTQ) teens say that doesn't paint a realistic portrait of all teens. So while your ideal may be that everyone should grow up, marry a person of the opposite sex, and have children, that may not reflect reality for your teen, your teen's friends, other family members, or the people she will meet throughout life.

Therefore, it makes sense to use gender-neutral terms whenever possible. Instead of telling your son, "One day you'll meet a great girl, fall in love, and marry her," you might go with a more general, "One day you'll meet someone you love deeply enough to make a lifelong commitment with." If your teen is GLBTQ, you'll be sending a message of inclusiveness and acceptance. If your teen is straight, you'll be creating an environment in which everyone can recognize and respect people who don't share their orientation or gender identity.

In recent decades, perceptions about gays and lesbians have changed (they have for transgender people, too, but the strides have not been as great). As the social stigma has started to fade, teens have increasingly felt comfortable coming out at younger and younger ages.

That means your own teen has a greater likelihood of encountering teens who openly identify as GLBTQ.

Whether or not your teen identifies as GLBTQ, it will help if you have an understanding of orientation and gender identity. Some of the more common terms:

Bisexual: Someone who has strong attractions to both men and women. She might be attracted more to one sex than the other or may feel equal attraction for both.

Coming out: Short for "coming out of the closet," or the process of telling others that you are gay or transgender. Someone who is "out" is open about his orientation or gender identity (although there are varying degrees of out—she might be out at home but not at work, for example).

Gay: A person (usually male) who is sexually or romantically attracted to someone of the same sex.

Gender identity: The way we identify our gender. It may be male, female, or transgender (below).

Heterosexual: A male or female who is sexually and/or romantically attracted to the opposite sex. "Straight" is another term used to mean heterosexual.

Homosexual: An outdated clinical term that is seen as derogatory by many in the gay community. Gay and lesbian are the preferred terms.

In the closet: Refers to someone who hides or fails to disclose his gender identity, sexual behavior, or orientation.

Lesbian: A female who is sexually and/or romantically attracted to other females.

Queer: Once a strictly derogatory term referring to all nonheterosexuals, it is now used proudly by some

GLBTQ people. It's not universally accepted, however, so it's better to steer clear of this one unless you're GLBTQ.

Questioning: Someone who is still determining her orientation or gender identity or does not identify with any particular label.

Sexual behavior: Refers to a person's sexual activities (and is different from orientation).

Sexual orientation: Refers to whom someone is sexually and/or romantically attracted, usually classified by gender. Orientations most commonly identified are straight, gay, bisexual, and lesbian.

Transgender: A person whose gender identity is different from his birth sex (a person with male genitals who identifies as female, or vice versa). Transgender people should be addressed and referred to with the pronoun that fits the gender they identify with.

ACCENTUATE THE POSITIVE

It's easy to focus on weak points: Your daughter may be too concerned about how she looks or spend too much time chatting online with her friends. Maybe you cringe at the sight of his bedroom, his choice in friends, or his complete lack of interest in current events.

Just remember that most teens' strong points outweigh whatever weaknesses they have—a fact that even they may overlook. In fact, teens often struggle with self-esteem; they are highly focused on how they're perceived by others and may find themselves falling short. They feel too flat-chested or too fat, not cool enough, not smart enough, too clumsy, too girly, not athletic enough—you know the drill.

And, research shows that teens with high self-esteem take better care of themselves physically and emotionally.

As a parent, you have many opportunities to enhance your teen's self-esteem. But to do so, you may need to look at your teen in a new light. It's easy to focus on those annoying tendencies —she spends an hour in the bathroom every morning attacking her natural curls with a flat iron and can't seem to pry herself away from her MySpace page long enough to communicate with you in person, for example. But, another look might reveal that she's diligent about taking care of her body and highly social.

Take a moment to think about your teen's strengths—write them down if it helps—and then think about that list when you talk to your teen. Some possibilities:

- responsible
- competent
- connected to community and friends
- loving
- sensitive to others' feelings
- decisive
- willing to stand up for beliefs
- persistent
- creative
- reasonable
- easygoing
- funny

Of course, that's not to say you should ignore the negatives. If your teen is spending three hours a night chatting with friends online instead of doing his homework for French class, you'll need to address that behavior.

But do acknowledge the positive. Saying, "I think it's so wonderful that you've developed such a tight-knit circle of friends," for example, puts the strengths first. At the same time, it gives you a jumping-off point for further discussion and encouragement of change, if it's needed.

Strive for the Seven Cs

It's all part of helping your teen become a healthy adult—one measure of which is resilience in the face of stressors. The American Academy of Pediatrics has identified seven characteristics of resilience.[4] The Seven Cs, as they're called, are:

Competence: The ability to handle situations effectively
Confidence: Belief in one's own abilities
Connection: Close ties to family, friends, school, and community
Character: A fundamental sense of right and wrong
Contribution: A sense of purpose and the desire to make choices that improve the world
Coping: The ability to cope effectively with challenges
Control: A sense of control over decisions and actions

The more teens—or anyone, for that matter—can master the Seven Cs, the better able they will be to cope with life's challenges. Help them do it, and you've given them skills that will last a lifetime.

Consider Temperament

Your teen may be happy, perky, and active. Or maybe you'd describe him as quiet, introspective, and aloof. You've probably noticed certain traits that have been evident since childhood; a baby who ate and slept on schedule and was always happy, for example, may have developed into an adolescent with a laid-back, cheerful attitude.

Temperament is a part of personality that is often defined simply as extroverted or introverted. But temperament is actually made up of many characteristics, including activity level, regularity, adaptability, emotional intensity, mood, distractibility, persistence, and sensitivity.

And although temperament can be affected by environment (a child who is easily distracted can be helped to improve his focus, for example), much of our temperament sticks with us for life. So don't be surprised if your emotionally intense daughter responds to a disappointment in a highly dramatic way or expect that your shy, introverted son will suddenly blossom into an outgoing teen who comes to you with every personal question that's on his mind.

As you consider the advice in this book, you'll need to take your teen's temperament into account. Will she open up and talk to you freely about feelings and emotions? Or is it more likely that you'll need to initiate—and work to maintain—a conversation? Does your teen's very nature make it difficult to talk to you about anything that's personal?

"Slow to warm up," shy teens who strive to get along and avoid conflict might seem easier to parent than impulsive, extroverted teens who thrive on asserting their independence. But the introverted teen might need additional guidance when it comes to peers and dating or asking an adult for help. And the extroverted teen may require a completely different approach—one that relies more on negotiation and parental monitoring. All of these are factors to consider when preparing to talk to your teen.

SET YOURSELF UP FOR SUCCESS

In real estate, location is everything. In comedy, it's timing. In communicating with your teen, it's a little of both. Ideally, you'll want to make sure your discussion happens in a place that's comfortable, private, and free from distractions, and at a time that's most likely to get a cooperative response.

Of course, you can't always control the environment. If you walk into your teenage son's bedroom and his girlfriend is lying naked in his bed, you won't have too much time to plan how and when to bring up the subject of sex (although, on the plus side, it certainly gives you a solid segue into a conversation about birth control and STI protection, as well as the rules of the house).

Or, if you're watching TV with your teenage daughter and a birth-control commercial comes on, your best bet is to grab the opportunity to talk rather than waiting to schedule a better time.

Still, there will be occasions when the timing is up to you. It can be extremely helpful to put a little thought into when and how such conversations happen. Some suggestions:

- **Allow time for cooling off.** If you stayed up all night waiting for your teen to get home (or slept in the recliner so you'd hear the key turning at 3 a.m.), you're probably angry and tired. It's all right to admit you're upset, but arrange a time later in the day to talk. You'll be a better communicator when you're rested and less likely to let your anger take over if you've had time to cool off.
- **Let her sleep.** Unless you have the rare teen who pops out of bed at the crack of dawn, perky and smiling, first thing in the morning isn't the best time for an effective conversation. Resist the urge to drag your teen out from under the covers so you can start the inquisition about last night's activities. Instead, wait until your teen has had time to wake up and get moving.
- **Find a quiet zone.** If your living room is a major thorough-fare—or home to the video game you can't get your teen's younger siblings to let go of—it's not the best place for a talk. Find a quiet spot that offers privacy and a break from interruptions.
- **Find a stable time.** Talking to teens about birth control the week before prom isn't a bad idea; talking to teens about it as they're getting ready to step into the limo is. Try to time your conversation so it doesn't correspond with upheaval or get lost in the shuffle of some bigger event.
- **Consider other options.** It's best if you can talk to your teen face to face, with plenty of eye contact and open body language. But if you (or your teen) are having a hard time talk-ing, avoiding a face-to-face sit-down might be a good option. Talking while you're driving can take some of the pressure off; you'll have to keep your eyes on the road. Talking in the dark (think: back porch in the moonlight on a summer night) might also let your teen speak up without fear of blushing.

You could also plan an activity so you can turn your eyes to something else while you talk. This works best if it's already part of your daily lives. If you garden together, bake, hike, canoe, whatever … you'll both have something else to focus on while you talk, which can lessen the discomfort of the face-to-face chat.

- **Cede a little control.** If you need to address a specific issue (such as a broken curfew) and you're sensing resistance, give your teen a choice of time to talk. Giving up control of one facet of the conversation can help head off your teen's feelings of being steamrolled.

Who Should Talk?

Generally speaking, conversations between parents and teens of the same gender are most comfortable. But unless one parent is completely uninvolved in your teen's life, it's ideal if both parents take part in ongoing discussions about sex. After all, each parent likely has important perspectives and experiences to share. Still, if your teen expresses a preference, the role of communicator-in-chief may fall to one parent.

If your teen isn't comfortable talking to either parent, broker a connection with a trusted third party—a minister, family friend, aunt or uncle, or health care worker—who can talk about issues related to sex and sexuality. Facilitate the meeting, but respect your teen's right to privacy by allowing the conversation to remain confidential. And do offer your teen future opportunities to talk to you. It might be as simple as saying, "I know you're talking to Uncle Joe about this, but I'm always here to talk if you need me." Leave that door open and your teen might just walk through it one day.

BEGINNING THE CONVERSATION

Ideally, you've been talking to your teen for years about the human body, sex, and sexuality—whether it was answering your three-year-old's question about why you have breasts or telling your preteen son he shouldn't be worried if he has wet dreams.

If you haven't talked to your teen much about sex and sexuality, don't panic. And don't let it stop you from opening up a conversation now. But since you're going to be boldly blazing a new path, you *should* acknowledge that you're breaking new ground and are doing it for a reason. After all, your teen is entering a momentous stage of life that calls for a new level of discussion. So talk about it. You might say: "You're reaching a time in your life when you're going to be faced with so many new experiences and will have to make some really adult decisions. It makes me realize that you and I probably need to talk about things more frankly than we have in the past. It might feel strange at first, but I think it's going to be really good for us both."

Your teen might be eager to hear from you—or resistant. Either way, you'll be doing your best to make sure he doesn't go it alone.

Once you start talking, you'll have to assume responsibility for keeping the conversation alive. Consider it part of your job and tackle it as you would any other important topic.

One Way to Say It ...

Mom:

It seems like this is uncomfortable for you to talk about with me.

Meg:

Yeah, it really is. And I already know this stuff from school.

Mom:

That's great. I know sex ed has been a good resource. But I think it's probably time for you to talk to your pediatrician about what's going on in your life. He can check you out and answer any questions you have that are specific to you.

Meg:

I guess that would be okay.

Mom:

> It's totally confidential. He won't tell me anything unless you say it's okay. And then, if you ever have any questions about stuff later on, you can always come to me. I'm here to talk whenever you need me. My biggest concern is that you're safe. If you're going to have sex, you need to protect yourself from pregnancy and disease, and even if you're not going to have sex now, you should be prepared for when you do. Okay?

Meg:

> Yeah, thanks.

Mom:

> And Meg, I'm always here if you have any questions or just want to talk.

Conversation Stoppers and Starters

Sometimes you really want to speak your mind. It's okay; you're only human, and along with the formation of opinions comes the desire to express them. This is especially true when it comes to the people we love and feel a responsibility toward. If you think your teen is making a poor decision, behaving badly, or not using common sense, it can be nearly impossible to bite your tongue.

But it *is* important to think before you speak and to avoid "conversation stoppers"—statements that are likely to kill a conversation. Generally, conversation stoppers are phrases that come across as sounding judgmental, dismissive, or insulting. A few to avoid:

- Don't be ridiculous (or silly).
- I can't believe you did that.
- What were you thinking?

- That was a stupid thing to do.
- Don't tell me you had sex with him.
- Don't come crying to me when you get pregnant.
- You really let me down.
- I'm so disappointed in you.
- You're embarrassing our family.
- You're too young to talk about this.
- You can't be serious.

If you do slip and utter a conversation stopper, a sincere apology can usually do wonders. Just stop, acknowledge what you said, identify it as a poor choice of words, and say, "I'm sorry." There's no need to give excuses beyond, perhaps, "I'm still trying to adjust to what you've told me," or "I was upset."

Going forward, think about how you can say things in a way that encourages conversation. Some words that usually work:

- I'm not sure I get it. Can you help me understand?
- I really want to know what you think.
- Can we talk about it?
- Your opinion matters to me.
- Tell me more.
- That's a good question.
- I'm so glad you came to me.
- I want to help you.
- Let's work through it together.

Defusing Your Teen's "Stoppers"
You should also be aware of (and prepared to react to) common conversation stoppers your teen might throw your way. Some examples:

The stopper: "I already know this stuff."
Your teen may well be informed about all things related to sex (although, as we discuss in chapter 4, you shouldn't rely solely on sex education at school to provide your teen with information).

However, you might point out that the purpose of talking with you is about more than just relating facts. Since it's your job to help make sure your teen stays safe, you need an open conversation. At the very least, your teen should talk to someone who can provide answers to personal questions in a private setting.

The stopper: "I don't want to talk."
If your teen doesn't want to talk to you, that's okay. Suggest another family member, doctor (offer to set up the appointment), or close family friend. But "I don't want to talk" might also mean, "I don't want to have the kind of conversation I think you're trying to have." Teens might automatically assume that a parent is going to lecture them about the dangers of sex or question them about their private lives. Explain that your goal is to make sure your teen is making safe and healthy decisions about sex. Teens who know a parent is serious about making it a nonjudgmental discussion—rather than a don't-do-it lecture—may be more willing to have a conversation.

The stopper: "I'm not having sex."
If you have evidence to the contrary or you strongly suspect that's not the truth, you can point it out. But do so as nonjudgmentally as possible. You might say, "I know that's what you say to me, but I also know there was a used condom in the toilet, and it wasn't mine." Try to avoid a power struggle; it won't accomplish your goal. You might follow up with an observation such as, "It seems as if this is really hard for you to talk about. Would you like me to make an appointment with your doctor so you can have a conversation with him in private?" Again, remind your teen that your chief concern is safety and that you're always available to talk.

The stopper: "It's my body, and I'll do what I want."
Again, avoid a power struggle by ceding the obvious. You might say, "You're right, it's your body and your choice. I can't force you to do something or not do something." But follow up with

an expression of your concerns. It might be, "I'm just worried that this isn't really something you want to do, and that maybe you're feeling pressured to have sex," or, "I want to make sure you're protecting yourself from pregnancy and STIs."

The stopper: Silence.

Silence can have many meanings, so you'll need to pause and tune in. Your teen may take your silence as an opportunity to open up. If not, restate your values and explain your concerns. If there's still no response, offer to put your teen in touch with someone else to talk to. And of course, be sure to give the reminder that you're always available as a resource.

Send a Message of Love and Respect

In any dealings with your teen—whether it's about sex or last night's homework—there are some basic guidelines for success. All are aimed at sending the message that you love and respect your teen and that you're there to help. Some of the basics:

Respect curiosity. No matter how silly the question, don't laugh. Instead, give praise for asking. "That's a good question," is a good place to start. Saying "don't be silly," or "why in the world would you think that?" is a surefire way to make sure your teen never comes to you with questions again. Even so, it's okay, and probably even a good idea, to smile when you talk to your teen about sex. You'll feel more relaxed and send the message that although it's a serious topic, it needn't be a dire one.

Respect privacy. Err on the side of caution when considering what to share with others. Even if you think something is too cute to keep to yourself—such as when your eleven-year-old asks if a girl can get pregnant from kissing—consider what you gain by sharing and what you stand to lose. If you think your teen would feel embarrassed, betrayed, or hurt by what you say to someone else, then zip your lips. And, unless there's a compelling safety reason that makes disclosure essential, you should always respect a teen's wishes that you not disclose something to another party.

Respect your teen's intelligence. If you don't know the answer, say so. It's not a contest. You don't have to be the smartest, most informed person in the world. But you do have to be the person in your teen's life who is most devoted to helping her find answers. Offer to find out or put your teen in touch with an expert who can.

Consider your commentary. Your teen has been learning from you since the day he was born, picking up clues along the way about your values and perspectives. Those clues may speak just as loudly—or even louder—than your carefully crafted messages. So, while you may say to your teen, "You can come to me with anything," if you deride the pregnant teenager down the street as being a slut or stupid, your teen will likely translate that to, "If that ever happens to me, my mom's going to think that about me."

If you know that you've already sent some conflicting messages, clarify them now. In the above example you might say, "I know I said something pretty mean about Carla when she got pregnant. I guess I was just shocked because she seems so young, and having sex at that age isn't something I think is appropriate." Then follow up with, "But I want you to know that I will always love you and that you can come to me with any problem, no matter what."

Think beyond the question. Younger teens especially may ask general questions about sex or the human body in an effort to determine whether they're normal. Or they may ask about "a friend" when they're really talking about themselves. You don't have to call them out on it—in fact, it's probably not helpful to— but you should think about what they're really looking for and try to deliver an answer that fits.

Remind them of your love. Even when teens do something that is contrary to a parent's values—and maybe especially then—it's important to remind them of your love, respect, and concern. If your teen did something you feel is "wrong," be clear that it's the behavior, and not the person, you object to. And, of course, one of the best ways to show your love is to stay involved in your teen's life.

LISTEN ACTIVELY

You may have practiced active listening before, but in the heat of an emotional conversation, it's easy to forget exactly what goes into good communication.

Active listening, or listening for meaning, can be a valuable tool in any communication. If you're listening actively, you have a better chance of making sure that you understand the meaning of what's being said. By confirming that what you heard is what was intended, you send the message that you're paying full attention to the discussion.

The first step in active listening is to focus on the conversation. That means getting rid of any distractions—whether it's the persistent beep coming from your laptop, your BlackBerry vibrating with the latest alert, or the old landline ringing off the hook. You can send the message that your teen has your undivided attention by silencing as many noises as possible.

It's common, especially with an emotional issue and in a parent-child relationship, to become so focused on what you want to say next that you miss what the other person is saying. In active listening, you work hard to focus on what the person is saying through her words, tone, and body language, and then you periodically state what you think you heard.

The beauty of active listening is that you don't have to agree—or even pretend to agree—with what the other party is saying. You're merely repeating the message you think the person is sending. By doing so, and asking for confirmation, you create an atmosphere of cooperation and make it more likely that the two of you can work together to find a middle ground.

Active listening reminders and tips:

- **Give him your full attention.** Turn off the gadgets, put down the paper, and face the speaker.
- **Be mindful of cues.** Note your teen's tone, word choice, body language, and other cues.
- **Acknowledge her emotions.** Say, "It seems like you're angry," or "You seem sad."
- **Encourage him to keep going.** Nod your head and offer phrases such as "I see," or "And then what did she say?"
- **Use a neutral tone.** Try to avoiding sounding shrill or angry, and avoid judgmental statements.
- **Ask open-ended questions.** Instead of "Were you sad that he didn't call yesterday?" try, "How did you feel when he didn't call?" This keeps your bias out of the equation and helps your teen establish her own feelings.
- **Paraphrase what you heard.** Say, "It sounds like you're saying," or "If I heard correctly," or "So what you're telling me is … "
- **Be honest.** If you don't understand, say so.
- **Listen to the response.** If your teen corrects your interpretation, listen to the additional information and try again.
- **Wait before coming to conclusions.** You'll only hear part of the message if you stop listening when your emotions kick in. Hear the speaker out.
- **Save your counterarguments for later.** Give your teen time to talk; wait to correct any falsehoods or respond to accusations until she's done.
- **Empathize.** Even if you disagree with your teen's statements, you can feel empathy for what she is feeling. "How painful for you," or "You probably wish she had told you that sooner" are two ways to express empathy.
- **Encourage your teen to consider solutions.** "What do you think would work best?" or "How can you make that happen?" might do the trick.
- **Offer to help.** It can be as simple as saying, "Is there anything I can do to help?"

Make Sure Your Teen Listens, Too

Since your teen may not have an adult's conversational skills, you may be the only party actively listening. Your teen, for example, may not hear you out, acknowledge your statements, or avoid judgmental statements. That makes it all the more important that you actively listen, but it also makes it a little more challenging for you.

You may want to give your teen a little leeway while standing your ground on certain rules of engagement. For example, you might let a teenager fail to hear you out because emotions are taking over. But don't allow your teen to cross the line into abusive language. Name-calling—on either party's part—should not be allowed.

Don't get involved in a shouting match or power struggle over whether you should even be having this conversation. Your teen will be unlikely to concede any point for fear of losing power. Instead, remind her that you expect to have an adult conversation because your teen is making adult choices that come with serious consequences. If such a conversation isn't possible now, put it on hold and reschedule it to give everyone time to cool off. You might say, "It seems like you're very angry right now, and it's hard for us to talk. I understand that, but this is a serious issue that we need to discuss. I think it's best if we talk this evening after dinner."

Now that you understand what's going on inside your teen, and what works best when talking to teens, you have a good start on the foundation you'll need to move forward in helping your teen. But you still don't have the whole picture. The world around us helps shape who we are. And since your teen's world is likely far different from the one you inhabited at the same age—just as teen life was different when you were young compared to your own parents' lives—your next step is to get a better understanding of just what it is that teens today are seeing, hearing, and doing.

CHAPTER 3

Media Madness, Hooking Up, and Friends with Benefits:
Today's Teenage World

If you've had relatively open communication as your teen moved from childhood to adolescence, you have a window into the world of today's adolescents. Maybe your daughter invited you to be her "friend" on Facebook—and you couldn't help but notice that she's "married" to her boyfriend of six months. Maybe your son sheepishly deflected your interest in his girlfriend with a coy, "We're just hanging out." Or perhaps you picked up some lingo on those long carpool rides, when backseat occupants giddily recount their day at school or weekend with friends.

Whatever the case, you've probably figured out that while you may not be the painfully out-of-touch geezer you always vowed not to become, some parts of teen life just aren't what they used to be.

The first step to understanding your teen's world is getting a clear picture of the messages teens get from the world at large and the impact those messages have. If you're living anywhere near a teenager, or even a preteen, you already know that even the geekiest among them—or perhaps especially the geekiest among them—are fully wired. Teens link to each other and the world in a way their parents could never have imagined. Not only do they have unprecedented access to communication tools— e-mail, instant messaging, social networking sites, and cell phones for talking and text messaging—but many can and do connect at all hours of the day. They may be instant-messaging friends with the latest gossip, texting their crush to arrange an impromptu meeting, or chatting on their always-on, always-handy cell phones.

And in the exhibitionist age of MySpace and Facebook, teens are increasingly accustomed to sharing almost every aspect of their lives with friends, acquaintances, and even complete strangers.

SEX IN THE MEDIA

Teens are also masters of the media: on average, they spend more than six and a half hours a day watching TV and movies, listening to music, playing video games, using a computer, and reading print publications.[5] Through it all, they are bombarded with sexual images and themes.

One example is TV, where the number of sexual scenes has nearly doubled since 1998.[6] Eleven percent of shows now depict sexual intercourse or strongly imply it. About half of the scenes that depict or imply intercourse involve characters in an established relationship, but 15 percent depict characters who have just met. And nearly 70 percent of shows include some sexual content, averaging five sex scenes an hour.

Little surprise then that when the National Campaign to Prevent Teen Pregnancy surveyed twelve- to nineteen-year-olds, 61 percent said the message they get from the media is that they're supposed to have sex. Similarly, 59 percent of teen girls said they often get the message that attracting boys and looking sexy is one of the most important things they can do.[7]

The Prevalence of Pornography

In addition to viewing sexual content on TV and in the movies, teens have greater access to pornography than any generation before them, thanks to the Internet. Not only is more porn available, but they have easy access to a broad range of pornographic material, which means they may be exposed to far more graphic displays than their parents likely encountered.

For the most part, young people don't view the availability of porn as a bad thing. In one study of 816 college students,[8] for example, researchers found that viewing porn was widely seen as acceptable behavior. Some 67 percent of young men (respondents were between eighteen and twenty-six years old) and 49 percent of women said viewing porn is acceptable, and 87 percent of young men and 31 percent of young women reported viewing pornography themselves. In this same age group, 48 percent of men and 3 percent of women said they view porn weekly. Even those who don't purposely seek it out may accidentally be exposed to porn as they stumble across websites or are sent adult content by spammers.

Just how much viewing porn affects the viewer is up for debate. Does watching porn create unrealistic expectations of sex for viewers? Does it encourage the mistreatment of women or sexual risk-taking? Does it reinforce the media's already skewed view of body shapes and sizes? Opinions vary.

Certainly porn doesn't usually portray healthy relationships between sexual partners. And although some adult content producers have incorporated condom use into their product, pornography overall isn't known for its promotion of safer sex. It also stands to reason that being exposed to a wider range of sexual activities may increase a person's likelihood of experimenting sexually. One Swedish study, for example, found a correlation between viewing porn and an increase in heterosexual anal sex among older teens.[9] But large-scale studies have yet to be completed. Until then, we can't say for sure how porn affects viewers' actual behavior.

It's fairly safe to say, though, that many teens will be exposed, either accidentally or on purpose, to pornography at some point. With that in mind, it makes sense to acknowledge the prevalence of pornography when talking to your teen, and to do so as part of your ongoing discussions about sex and sexuality (which, remember, ideally would have started long before your teen had sex). When you do talk, be sure to:

- Talk about your values. You may feel that viewing any porn is wrong, that only some porn crosses the line, or that all porn is okay for people of a certain age. Tell your teen how you feel and why.

- Discuss the fact that pornography often doesn't paint a realistic portrait of sex, of relationships between men and women, and of the dangers of unprotected sex.
- Talk to your teen about your rules for computer use and other relevant rules of the house (see chapter 7 for more on rules).

Sexy Gets Younger

If you look at the world through a teen's eyes, it's easy to see why girls, in particular, might be confused. On the one hand they're told by parents, teachers, and other well-meaning adults that they are competent, capable, and valued for all that they have to give the world, regardless of how they look or dress.

On the other hand, they're bombarded by a conflicting message—that looks matter most, that girls and women are sexual objects to be coveted, and that men and boys are sexually insatiable. Objectifying women is nothing new, but the sexualization of younger and younger girls in recent years is ringing alarm bells among child advocates and psychologists.

Girls are increasingly portrayed in the media (in advertising, movies, TV programming, and video games) in provocative poses or clothing, or presented as objects to be coveted. They are often depicted as—and encouraged to appear—more adultlike than their years (while older women are encouraged to appear more youthful). Girls are hammered with marketing that was once aimed squarely at adults—from G-strings for preteens to vampy Halloween costumes for middle schoolers (with parents and even grandparents playing accomplice by footing the bill).

WHEN SEXY ISN'T GOOD

A task force formed by the American Psychological Association studied the issue in 2006 and found that sexualization of girls can actually hinder cognitive performance. It referenced tests in which girls who were focused on appearance actually had greater difficulty with mathematical tasks and logical reasoning. Sexualization can also lead to a host of health problems, including eating disorders, low self-esteem, and depression. There's even an impact on sexual health. Girls who see themselves as sexual objects may not be as sexually assertive and may be less likely to insist their partner wear a condom during sex, the study authors said.

The hip-hop culture in particular has come under fire for its portrayal of women and focus on sex. In fact, studies of the genre point to some interesting distinctions. One study found that sexual lyrics—crooning about the urge to have sex, for example—don't increase the likelihood of early sexual encounters, but sexually degrading lyrics do.[10] Such lyrics depict women as sexual objects and men as sexually insatiable. (It's important to note, however, that teens who are most interested in sex may be the ones who tend to listen to such music, which would skew the results of such a study.)

What's a parent to do? Should you toss the TV? Ban teen magazines or outlaw outings to the local dance club? As tempting as that might be, bans aren't likely to help, given the pervasiveness of media and the unswerving drive of adolescents to experience the adult world. Still, especially for young teens, it's worthwhile to limit your teen's exposure to unhealthy images and messages. And you should, whenever possible, challenge such messages and images. Speak up. You're modeling behavior your teen can emulate.

Teen Targeted: The P-Word, And More

Under 15: If you haven't already, talk to your teen about pornography. Point out that porn doesn't paint a realistic portrait of sex, relationships, or the average human body (and see chapter 7 for setting rules on Internet use). Limit exposure to sexually degrading lyrics that portray women as sexual objects. Look for teachable moments in the form of news stories, TV shows, music videos, or song lyrics to talk to your teen about sexual stereotypes and how they can hurt.

15 to 17: Your ability to limit exposure is waning, but you can still challenge unhealthy stereotypes and present your own values for your teen to evaluate. As always, start talking to your teen about it when the moment seems right.

18 and over: Your teen is old enough to establish her own values and make her own decisions about right and wrong. Let her. But be available for thoughtful, adult conversations about sex and the media.

EVERYONE'S DOING IT, RIGHT?

Considering pop culture's focus on sex and sexuality—and the natural tendency of parents to fear the worst—you could be forgiven for thinking teens are more sexually active today than in generations past.

But are they more likely to have sex than their counterparts fifteen years ago? The answer is probably not. Teen sexual activity, which rose steadily in the decades leading up to the 1990s, saw a significant drop between 1990 and 2001, after which it has plateaued.[11]

By 2001, the percentage of high schoolers who'd had inter-course at least once dropped to 46 percent, compared to 54 percent ten years earlier. By 2007, the number had risen slightly to 48 percent.[12]

Not surprisingly, older teens are more likely than younger teens to have had sex. By age group, sexual activity breaks down like this:

- 65 percent of 12th graders have had sex at least once.
- 56 percent of 11th graders have had sex at least once.
- 44 percent of 10th graders have had sex at least once.
- 33 percent of 9th graders have had sex at least once.
- 17 percent of 7th and 8th graders have had sex at least once.[13]

In addition, teens today are more likely to delay their sexual debut than teens did fifteen years ago. In 2002, some 13 percent of girls and 15 percent of boys aged fifteen to nineteen reported they'd had sex before age fifteen, compared with 19 percent and 21 percent, respectively, in 1995.[14] By 2002, the average teen reported having sex for the first time at age seventeen (although some experts caution that figure may be misleading because it doesn't include teens who aren't attending school and those who are past their first half of senior year).

What we know about the first sexual encounter:

- About 7 percent of teens say they were younger than thirteen when they first had sex.
- Fifteen percent of adults say they abstained from sex until they were twenty-one years of age.
- The majority of girls (59 percent) had a sexual partner who was one to three years older, although 8 percent had first partners who were six or more years older.[15]
- Sixty percent of sexually experienced teens aged twelve to nineteen say they wish they'd waited longer to have sex for the first time.[16]

Keep in mind, though, that just because a teen has had sex doesn't mean she is sexually active. Of those who reported having sex, only 35 percent said they'd done so in the past three months, with older teens being more likely than younger ones to be sexually active.[17] That may be because they don't have a regular partner—as you would in, say, a marriage—but also because they've decided after their first encounter to wait until they're older to have sex again.

One more positive trend to note: Teens today report slightly fewer partners than they did in 1991. In 2005, about 14 percent of teens reported they'd had sexual intercourse with more than four partners, compared with 19 percent in 1991. Boys were more likely to have had more than four partners—16.5 percent of boys said they'd had four or more partners, while 12 percent of girls said the same.

Parents: The Anti-Risk

Generally speaking, the teens most likely to delay sex are those who have a feeling of connectedness to family, who are supervised, who take part in activities with family, and whose parents have high expectations for school success and behavior.[18] Teens who reported a close bond with their mothers and whose mothers clearly communicated their values also were more likely to delay having sex for the first time.[19]

Other factors have an impact, too. Teens with strong religious beliefs are more likely to delay sex, as are teens whose parents talk to them about delaying sexual activity. In general, teens living with both parents, and whose parents have higher education and income levels, are more likely to postpone sexual intercourse.[20]

And although school may seem like a hormonal hotbed, greater involvement in school, including sports and after-school activities, is related to postponing sex and less sexual risk-taking. Schools, after all, structure teens' time, help select their social group, and put them in constant contact with adults in the form of teachers and administrators who discourage unhealthy risk-taking.

Schools are also where many (but not all) teens are taught sex education, which can be a factor in whether or not teens decide to have sex. In fact, teen girls were 59 percent less likely to start having sex before age fifteen if they had sex education, while teen boys were 71 percent less likely.[21] Once they do have sex, teens who've taken sex education are less likely to participate in risky behaviors such as unprotected sex and sex with multiple partners (although what kind of sex education they get is also important, as we'll discuss in chapter 4).

Teen Targeted: Sexual Norms and Decision Making

Under 15: Teens of all ages have misconceptions about who is doing what, and at what age. They may think, "Everyone's doing it," and while it's unwise to say that no one is (that whopper won't pass the teen sniff test), it's a good idea to talk honestly about sexual norms. Discuss the average age of first intercourse (roughly at age seventeen) and the fact that most teens, especially younger teens, who've had sex once aren't sexually active. You might mention the 60 percent of teens who wish they'd waited. Talk about the reasons teens might feel that way. If you believe it's better to wait to have sex, say why.

15 to 17: Key talking points include the average age of first intercourse, the fact that most teens who've had sex aren't sexually active, and the fact that teens with clear goals are more likely to delay sex. Talk to your teen about his goals and about how the decisions he makes—including decisions about sex—can impact those goals.

18 and over: Your teen is likely near or at a critical point in life: the end of high school. Talk to her about goals and dreams and how decisions—including decisions about sex—can impact those goals.

Virginity Pledges: Do They Work?

Studies show that virginity pledges do work to some degree. Teens who make these promises tend to delay having sex, on average, by eighteen months. But teens who make such pledges might be more inclined to wait anyhow, either for religious or personal reasons, and 88 percent of pledgers do have sex before marriage.

And when they do have sex for the first time, teens who made virginity pledges are less likely to use contraception and are just as likely as their non-pledging counterparts to contract a sexually transmitted infection.

That doesn't mean you should discourage your teen from making a virginity pledge if he is so inclined. Abstinence, after all, is the only surefire way to avoid an unplanned pregnancy and STIs. Applaud your teen's commitment. But don't close the file on your teen's sexuality or assume there's no need to provide information about birth control and STI prevention. Continue talking so that you can be a resource, should your teen need you.

TEENS AND ORAL SEX

One thing in particular strikes fear in the hearts of parents—the thought of teenage girls indiscriminately offering oral sex to every boy they meet. It all started with rumors of so-called rainbow parties, where girls wearing different shades of lipstick work their way down a line of boys, performing oral sex, and contributing to the lipstick rainbow as they go. In 2003, the press—from the *Oprah Winfrey Show* to major media outlets—picked up the story and ran with it, stoking fears as they went.

So, were the parties—which were also dubbed "chicken parties" for the way girls' heads supposedly bobbed as they performed oral sex—real? Were teenage girls actually servicing their middle-school classmates en masse at the back of the bus, in basement rec rooms, and anywhere else they could get their hands on each other? Or was it all urban legend and parental panic? The answer is probably somewhere in the middle.

Although there are a few high-profile anecdotes of group oral sex encounters among young teens, more than five years later there is no evidence that such encounters are happening with any regularity.

Still, it's worth noting that teens are, indeed, engaging in oral sex. In the National Survey of Family Growth, a U.S. government survey conducted in 2002, about 55 percent of boys and 54 percent of girls aged fifteen to nineteen reported that they'd had oral sex with someone of the opposite sex.[22] About 12 percent had had oral sex but not vaginal intercourse.

The actual numbers of teens who have oral sex weren't a big change from a similar survey conducted in 1995, but unfortunately there are no good statistics before 1995 to show definitively whether teens are having oral sex more today than they were years ago. And we don't have solid numbers on what has happened since 2002. We also don't have much context for the numbers that we do have. Did teens have oral sex in the context of a relationship? Were they doing it in a group or alone, and with just one partner? Did they have oral sex and then "progress" to vaginal sex or vice versa? We simply don't know, although a recent analysis of 2002 data points to the likelihood that teens seem to jump into a range of sexual activities—including oral and vaginal sex—at about the same time.[23] That seems to debunk the myth that teens have flocked to oral sex as a way to technically remain virgins.

But it is becoming increasingly clear that today's teens probably don't view oral sex in the same way their parents, and most certainly their grandparents, did. Where oral sex was once seen as intensely intimate and even a little risqué—a step up in seriousness from intercourse, for some—it has largely been demystified to the point of the commonplace.

Casual Attitudes and Negative Feelings

Part of the casual attitude toward oral sex may be rooted in the emergence of HIV and in teens' increased access to information about safer sex. Since there's no risk of pregnancy and a reduced risk of some STIs, many people consider oral sex a safer alternative to intercourse. In fact, in one study, teens said they do see oral sex as safer than intercourse—both physically and emotionally—and that even when the partners are not dating, oral sex is more acceptable than intercourse for their age group.[24]

But while oral sex might, in some cases and in some ways, be safer than intercourse, there are physical and emotional risks that teens often fail to consider. On the physical side, many STIs can be passed via oral sex. On the emotional side, a study of ninth- and tenth-grade students in California found that girls were twice as likely to feel bad about themselves after oral sex than boys (boys were more likely to say it gave them a boost in confidence and popularity).[25]

Overall, 41 percent of boys and girls said they felt bad about themselves later, with 20 percent saying they felt guilty and 25 percent saying they felt "used." Teens who had oral sex but not intercourse reported less guilt and fewer worries about STIs and pregnancy than those who had vaginal intercourse, but they also reported less pleasure, self-confidence, and intimacy with their partner.

Quick Stats: Oral Sex

- More than half of all teens have had oral sex.
- Seventy percent of eighteen- and nineteen-year-olds have had oral sex.
- Male and female teens report similar rates of giving and receiving oral sex.

You Call *That* Sex?

Are you still a virgin if you have oral sex? What about anal sex? Can you say you're "abstinent" if you do either? You might be surprised to hear how teens interpret these terms.

In one of the biggest recent studies done on the topic,[26] when teens were asked to define virginity, 94 percent of teens considered vaginal intercourse to be the act that leads to lost virginity. Asked whether they'd consider someone to have lost his or her virginity after certain acts, here's what they said:

- Genital touching: 84 percent said no
- Oral sex: 71 percent said no*
- Anal sex: 16 percent said no

*Some teens might quibble on oral sex, calling it sex only if orgasm occurred.

In general, teens tend to view abstinence even more broadly. While virginity is a one-time prospect (once you lose it there's no going back), teens view the idea of abstaining from sex more fluidly. They may consider themselves to be abstinent if they haven't had sexual activity in several months, for example. And they may consider themselves abstinent even if they've participated in certain sexual behaviors. For example, when asked what type of behavior could be considered abstinent:

- 24 percent of teens said anal sex
- 37 percent of teens said oral sex
- 60 percent said touching another person's genitals until he or she reaches orgasm

Teen Targeted: Protected Sex

Under 15: Generally, younger teens are more likely than older teens to include touching and other acts, such as deep kissing, as "sex." The same can be said for less sexually experienced teens, as compared with their more sexually experienced counterparts. Talk about it. Ask your teen specifically what he means by "sex." Then make sure your teen is prepared to prevent pregnancy and the spread of STIs.

15 to 17: Teens in this age group are more likely to be sexually experienced, but they still may not be well informed. When you talk about sex, be sure to define it. This is especially true when you're talking about pregnancy prevention and STI protection. If you say, "Use a condom when you have sex," and your teen doesn't consider anal sex to be "sex," you've got a problem.

18 and over: Teens of this age likely know more about pregnancy prevention and STI protection, but there still may be cultural factors that result in you and your teen having different definitions of sex. When in doubt, clarify what you mean. It may be as simple as choosing your words carefully, so instead of "Use a condom when you have sex," you might go with, "Use a condom any time you're having intimate contact with someone, whether it's oral sex, anal sex, vaginal intercourse, or anything else that involves close contact with genitals or bodily fluids." Yes, we know, it's awkward to spell it all out. But clarity trumps comfort in this case.

Go Ahead, Say It ...

If you cringe every time you think of uttering the words "anal sex" to your teen, we feel your pain. For most parents, it's not a phrase that rolls off the tongue. And, let's face it, you might not have a much easier time with penis, vagina, or vaginal intercourse.

But don't be tempted to omit anal sex (or any other uncomfortable words) when you talk to your teen. As much as you might have trouble putting it into words, people do have anal sex. In fact, 11 percent of teens report engaging in anal sex with someone of the opposite sex.[27] And by the time they turn twenty-four, 34 percent of men and 32 percent of women have had heterosexual anal sex (by age forty-four the numbers are 40 percent for men and 35 percent for women). Although there's no risk of pregnancy with anal sex, the act does come with an increased risk of STIs, especially HIV (we'll talk more about that in chapter 5), so it's important to address.

Your job will be easier if you've spoken openly with your teen about the human body all along (steering clear of cutesy nicknames and calling genitals by their proper names when your child is young helps set the stage for later matter-of-fact discussions about the body and sex). But if you haven't, now is a good time to start. Or at least to practice. Go ahead and say "vagina" (unless you're reading this on the bus, in the waiting room at the doctor's office, or some other place where you'll be met with raised eyebrows. Trust us, that's not going to go over well). Say it with confidence. And now "penis." And finally, "anal sex." Go ahead, you're on a roll.

And if you really, really can't—or if your effort is so obviously painful that it will make your teen shudder on your behalf—then make sure you connect your teen with a doctor or other health care provider who will talk about the full range of sexual activities (see chapter 4 for more on what type of doctor to look for and what to look for in a doctor).

Why Do It? (Why Not?)

The why of sex might seem obvious: It feels good, for one. And it's one way to express love for a partner. Still, people's reasons for engaging in sex can vary—and they're not always good. Some examples of the not-so-good:

- because you're under pressure from your partner, friends, or anyone else
- to feel cool or adult
- to lose your virginity
- to hang on to a partner
- to make someone else feel good, even though it doesn't make you feel good

If your teen is sexually active, talk to him or her about his or her decision to have sex. Some teens will find that in trying to explain their reasoning to someone else, they gain insight into the situation themselves. But don't be entirely surprised if your teen can't identify a reason. For some teens, becoming sexually active involved very little thought or planning; others simply won't be able to put it into words. Your effort isn't in vain, however. Simply considering the question may offer your teen some benefit and insight into the decision-making (or lack of decision-making) process and the outcome.

FRIENDS WITH BENEFITS

As you've read, the good news is that teens are delaying their sexual debut and have fewer sexual partners in their teenage years than they did fifteen years ago.

What they're not doing is waiting to have sex until they're married. In fact, 95 percent of Americans have sex before marriage (and 81 percent do so before they turn twenty).[28] That's perfectly logical—and not necessarily a problem, depending on your values—given that Americans on average are marrying later than in years past (the average age is now twenty-five for women and twenty-seven for men). The delay in marriage means that people today spend more time as single, sexually mature adults.

But they haven't sworn off all commitment. In fact, more than three-quarters of teenage girls say their first sexual experience was in the context of a committed relationship—either with a steady boyfriend, fiancé, or husband.

Clearly, though, the expectations surrounding sex and relationships have changed over the years. Today about 50 percent of women and 60 percent of men think it's okay for unmarried eighteen-year-olds to have sex as long as they have "strong affection" for one another. There's notably less support for younger teens, however. Only 20 percent of men and 13 percent of women say sex between two unmarried sixteen-year-olds is okay.[29]

The relationships themselves have changed, too. Although sex between friends is hardly a new phenomenon, today's teen culture has formalized relationships that tie friendship—but not romantic feelings—with sex.

They're called friends with benefits (FWBs), and the "benefit" is sex, with the expectation that two friends will share it without a romantic involvement. Friends with benefits might hook up on occasion (or frequently), but there's no long-term commitment. They may have fun together, talk, and hang out, but they typically don't go on dates, don't feel obligated toward each other in any romantic way, and don't act like a couple in public.

Sometimes good friends will be FWBs just for the mutual physical pleasure. Other times a sexually active couple will downgrade to FWBs while they transition out of their romance, still hooking up on occasion but with the unspoken understanding that the committed part of the relationship is over. Sometimes FWBs are just casual acquaintances who don't even have much of a "friend" relationship to build on. In most cases they wouldn't necessarily commit to being FWBs in so many words—and don't negotiate or talk about the terms of the relationship—but such a setup would be clearly recognizable as an FWB arrangement.

A guaranteed hookup may sound good if you're a teen in search of sex without strings. But the FWB dynamic only works well if both parties share the same nonromantic feelings for each other. If not, the arrangement is likely to be extremely unsatisfying to at least one party. And there's evidence that although the term is used by both genders, girls and boys typically interpret it in different ways.

In one study, of the 60 percent of college students who reported they'd been in an FWB relationship, female respondents were more likely to report being emotionally involved while male respondents were more likely to be sexually focused. Male respondents also were more likely to report having more than one FWB relationship going at once.[30]

Another study of 125 young men and women at Michigan State University found that FWB relationships most often ended amicably, but not romantically.[31] About 36 percent of those who had been in an FWB relationship said the relationship stopped being sexual, but that they remained friends. Twenty-eight percent said they stayed friends and remained sexually active; 26 percent said they were no longer friends (or sexual partners), and just 10 percent said the relationship graduated to a traditional dating relationship.

That there is such a relationship at all may be surprising to some parents. But other dating arrangements won't be. "Going steady" and even "going with" are no longer the terms of choice in most circles, but the relationship itself still exists, for example. Most teens would just call it dating, although teens might also say they're "talking to" or "hanging out with" another teen they're casually dating (although both can also have entirely casual, friendly connotations).

If you're feeling a little out of touch, you might find some comfort in the fact that the term *hooking up* is still around, with its meaning largely unchanged. Generally speaking up, hooking up means engaging in any sexual or romantic act, from kissing, to petting, to oral sex, anal sex, or intercourse (although, again, it can also have nonsexual meaning). If you're not sure about other relationship terms, see the list at the end of this chapter (but use them cautiously; coming from your lips, "booed up" is likely to sound as ridiculous to your teen as it does to you).

GLBT or Q?

It's not uncommon for teens to have sexual thoughts about someone of the same gender, and it's also common for them to feel freaked out when they do. It's part of the natural process of exploring ourselves as sexual beings. But such thoughts can be confusing, especially for young teens, who may be overwhelmed by all the changes in their lives. It may be nothing more than a teen's brain working through the maze of sexual feelings, or it could be a sign that a teen is attracted to the same sex or has a nontraditional gender identity.

Since the teenage years are a time of experimentation, acting on those thoughts isn't necessarily a sign of anything other than, well, experimentation. Teens may dabble with same-sex encounters as they try to figure out who they are sexually, what they like, and what their sexual identity will be. They may turn out to be straight even if they've had same-sex encounters, and they may turn out to be gay even if they've had opposite-sex encounters. Teens may also explore different gender identities.

Some will feel certain they know their orientation or identity; others will find it's too soon to tell.

To put it in perspective, here are a few stats on orientation:[32]

- There are no solid data on how many teens are GLBTQ, but experts generally assume the prevalence to be around one in ten teens.
- 4 percent of men and women aged eighteen to forty-four say they are gay or bisexual.
- 11 percent of women aged eighteen to forty-four have had at least one same-sex sexual experience in their lifetime, up from 4 percent in a similar survey conducted in 1992 (although the rise may have more to do with greater comfort in admitting such behavior than an increase in the behavior itself).
- 6 percent of males aged fifteen to forty-four have had oral sex with another male.
- 4 percent of males aged fifteen to forty-four have had anal sex with another male.

Although stigma and peer pressure still exist, acceptance of gays, lesbians, and bisexuals has seen a steady rise in recent decades. In 2006, for example, 54 percent of Americans said they consider it acceptable to be gay, compared to 38 percent in 1992, according to Gallup polls.

Still, although perceptions have improved, GLBTQ teens still face harassment and violence, a reality every parent should be aware of (see chapter 8 for more on this).

Under the Influence: Sex, Drugs, and Alcohol

If you've ever been drunk or high, you know that alcohol and drugs can reduce inhibitions, making you more likely to do things you wouldn't if you were sober. That applies to sex, and teens are no exception.

In 2005, 22.5 percent of teens said they were under the influence of drugs or alcohol the last time they had sex.[33] Teens who use drugs or alcohol are more likely to get involved in other risky behavior, including unprotected or high-risk sex.

If you're thinking "my teen doesn't do that," you may be right. But you might also consider that alcohol and even some drug use is fairly common, especially among teens. A breakdown of teen drug use by age:[34]

12th graders reporting drug use:

Marijuana: 32 percent
Ecstasy: 4.5 percent
Cocaine: 8 percent
Alcohol (in past 30 days): 44 percent

10th graders reporting drug use:

Marijuana: 25 percent
Ecstasy: 3.5 percent
Cocaine: 5 percent
Alcohol (in past 30 days): 33 percent

8th graders reporting drug use:

Marijuana: 10 percent
Ecstasy: 3 percent
Cocaine: 3 percent
Alcohol (in past 30 days): 16 percent

The European View

In the United States, parents who learn that their teen is sexually active tend to worry. What if he gets someone pregnant? What if she gets an STI? What if my teen is just not mature enough to handle such an adult act? Sometimes it's just a niggling concern; sometimes it's flat-out panic.

In western Europe, that's typically not the case. There, sex among unmarried teens is widely accepted as the norm. And although you might guess that teens who are given the green light to have sex are more likely to get pregnant or have STIs, you'd be wrong. The United States has a far higher rate of teen pregnancy and STI infection than most of western Europe, as well as a much higher incidence of abortion.

In the Netherlands, Germany, and France, intimate sexual relationships are seen as a natural part of a person's development into a sexually healthy adult. Mass-media campaigns, public health systems, and education policies there emphasize sex within the confines of a committed relationship and individual responsibility for STI and pregnancy prevention. This compares to a much more conflicted approach in the United States, where teen sex is often portrayed as deviant behavior and, therefore, something that should be suppressed or hidden.

As a result, although teens in the United States are just as likely to have sex, they're less likely to do so responsibly. Many youth sexual health advocates suggest—and we concur—that parents try to emulate the European model when thinking about how to approach teen sexuality.

Say What?

Chances are that when they speak to you, teens don't use the same words they'd use with their friends. Your teen speaks and, for the most part, you understand. But if you sat in on a conversation your fifteen-year-old son had with his buddies, you'd be a little lost.

How teens talk, and what they say, varies greatly depending on the culture they most identify with and what they're exposed to socially and through the media. Suburban teens might not adopt exactly the same language as their urban counterparts. Teens who are into the hip-hop scene will talk differently than teens who love country music.

You can't hope to know it all. And really, it wouldn't help much if you did. But you should at least be aware of common terms (although, as we mentioned before, don't be tempted to adopt their language—you won't gain any credibility; trust us).

Some terms related to sex and relationships:

Bi-curious: Curious about gay or lesbian sex or about engaging in same-sex activities

Blow job: Oral sex performed on a male; also called fellatio, among other things

Bobblehead: A female who gives oral sex

Bone: A verb describing sex (usually in reference to a male having sex)

Boo: Boyfriend for girlfriend

Booed up: Spending a lot of time with a significant other

Booty call: A phone call, instant message, text message, or other form of contact, usually late at night, aimed at arranging a sexual hookup. The term can also refer to the person who is the object of the call, as in "he's my booty call."

Bop: A name given to a girl known for giving oral sex

Bopper: someone (female) who sleeps with other girls' boyfriends

Brain: Blow job or oral sex

Candy: Can refer to drugs or can be a code word for sex

Chicken head: Usually refers to a girl who is known for giving oral sex

Chicken party: A party where a single girl or group of girls performs oral sex on a group of boys (how often this happens is probably exaggerated)

Chopping: Having sex often

Crush: A strong attraction (typically undeclared). Can also refer to the person you're attracted to

Cup cakin': Flirting with or being obviously affectionate with

Cut buddy: See Friends with benefits

Cut party: See Chicken party. Also could refer to a party where several people have sex

Cutting: Having sex

Extended hookup: See Friends with benefits

Friends with benefits: Friends who have sex with each other on a regular basis but aren't in a committed relationship. Also called pals with privileges, cut friends, cut buddies, friends with privileges, or sex buddies, among other things. The relationship might also be called an extended hookup or a fling

Hanging out: Spending time with someone in a nonromantic way. Can also refer to casual dating or just spending time with someone (as a friend)

Hookup: A casual, intimate encounter that can involve anything from kissing to sex. Hooking up can also have nonsexual connotations. A "hookup" can also refer to the person you hook up with

Jockin' or Sweatin': Pursuing someone aggressively

Rainbow party: A gathering where a succession of girls performs oral sex on a boy or several boys. So-called because the girls wear different colored lipstick, leaving a "rainbow" of colors on the boy's penis (how often this happen is probably exaggerated)

Rimming: Also called anilingus, a rim-job, and salad tossing, among other things; rimming refers to anal-oral contact

Roller: Someone who sleeps around

Sext: Sending a sexually explicit image, usually via cell phone

Talking to: Can mean the early stages of dating. Usually used after two people have had one date but aren't actually dating yet

Technical virgin: Someone who has participated in oral or anal sex or mutual masturbation but not vaginal intercourse

You Matter. Seriously.

When your thirteen-year-old rolls her eyes or tunes you out and turns up the volume on her iPod, it might feel like you're talking to a wall. But studies show that teens actually do care what their parents think. In fact, when asked who influences them most in decisions about sex, 47 percent of teens point to their parents.[35]

After parents, teens say they're influenced by friends, themselves, and religious leaders, respectively. Only 3 percent of teens say the media is influential, compared to 10 percent of adults who say the media influences teens most.[36]

Teens also say they mostly base their decisions about having sex on their values and sense of right and wrong.[37] But for parents who worry that their own values message has been lost in the fray, there's good news. The majority of teens say they share their parents' values (and only a tiny fraction say they don't know their parents' values.)[38]

Even so, parents may be giving themselves higher marks for being candid about sex than their teens think they deserve. Far more parents say they talked to their teens about sex than teens report, which means either parents are fudging the numbers or their teens aren't counting parents' ineffective attempts to broach the subject.

What does it all mean? First, you shouldn't underestimate your influence. Second, you shouldn't assume your teen won't talk or listen. Use the tips outlined in this book to open and then continue a running discussion with your teen.

CHAPTER 4

Sex Ed:
Teen Pregnancy, STIs, and
Birth Control

I f your teen has had sex education in school, you might
be content to sit back and let the teacher handle the tricky
talk—you know, the part about STIs, birth control,
and pregnancy.

And you may be right in assuming your teen is learning
something about sex in school. The vast majority of children in
public schools do get some form of sex education. That's good
news because research shows that teens who have formal sex
education before they start having sex are more likely to delay
intercourse and are less likely to report a teen pregnancy than
those who have no sex education.

But not all sex ed classes are equal. Some provide information about birth control and condoms, some don't. Because of
the rise of abstinence-only-until-marriage education in the past
decade, one in three teens today gets no formal education about
birth control or condoms.[39] Only about 66 percent of boys and
70 percent of girls today receive formal instruction about birth
control, compared to 81 percent of boys and 87 percent of girls
in 1995.[40]

ABSTINENCE PROGRAMS

Many schools in the United States today provide what's dubbed "abstinence-plus," a curriculum that promotes abstinence as the only surefire way to prevent pregnancy and STIs, while at the same time providing information about birth control and STI protection. Such programs have been shown to be effective in delaying teens' sexual debut and in increasing the likelihood that they'll use birth control and condoms when they do have sex.

But since the mid-1990s, a growing number of school districts have switched to abstinence-only-until-marriage education, mainly due to increased federal funding aimed at promoting such programs (since 1996 the federal government has spent about $1 billion on such funding).

To get government funding for abstinence-only-until-marriage programs, states must follow a rigid set of rules, such as teaching that the "expected standard" for human sexual activity is "a mutually faithful, monogamous relationship in the context of marriage" and that sex outside of marriage is likely to have harmful psychological and physical effects. The rules prohibit discussion of birth control and condoms, except to emphasize failure rates.

Abstinence-Only Doesn't Work

Critics have long decried abstinence-only education, saying the focus on sex within the context of marriage not only excludes most GLBTQ teens but also is unrealistic for the vast majority of teens. They point to the fact that 95 percent of Americans have sex before marriage, and 81 percent do so before they turn twenty.[41] Programs that don't teach about condoms and birth control—or that emphasize failure rates—also put teens in danger for unplanned pregnancies and STIs.

In 2007, a federally funded study of four abstinence-only programs found the programs to be ineffective—

teens not only failed to abstain from sex but there also was no effect on the age at which teens first had sex or how many partners they had.[42]

Other studies have found similar results (although one study showed short-term gains for some programs). One study found that teens who had comprehensive sex education had a 50 percent lower risk of teen pregnancy than those who received abstinence-only education.[43]

And the programs themselves have taken hits for distorting facts. When one group reviewed the thirteen most commonly used courses, it found that only two were accurate, while eleven others, which were widely used in many states, were seriously flawed.

As a result of such studies, states increasingly are refusing federal funds for abstinence-only education, which may mean its days are numbered.

PARENTAL ACTION ITEMS

However, there are steps you can take to make sure your teen is getting the information she needs:

- **Be informed.** Don't assume your teen is getting comprehensive sex ed in school. Check with your teen's school to find out exactly what the course covers and when it's offered. Teaching teens about condoms and birth control is most effective if it's done before a teen starts having sex, so your teen should be taking an age-appropriate course as early as possible. (Unfortunately, nearly half of boys and 40 percent of girls say they didn't get information about birth control and STI protection before they first had sex.)

- **Talk to teens about what they know.** Your teen may identify areas he would like to learn more about or tell you more about what's being taught at school.
- **Supplement.** Even teens who are getting a comprehensive sex education at school likely have questions that relate to their particular situation. Make sure your teen has every chance possible to find answers to questions (and, yes, assume all teens have questions … it's a rare teen who doesn't). Buy a good book, talk to your teen about sex, and find a doctor or other medical professional who can answer questions.
- **Advocate for change.** If you're not happy with what's being taught, or when it's being taught, take steps to effect change. The Sexuality Information and Education Council of the United States (SIECUS) is one group that advocates for comprehensive sex education in schools. Its website, www.siecus.org, includes information about becoming an advocate in addition to resources on sex and sex education.

FEARS AND REALITY: TEEN PREGNANCY

When parents find out or suspect their teen is sexually active, they may be disappointed that their teen hasn't adopted their own values, but they're also faced with very real fears, both rational and irrational, about the dangers their teen may face.

Just what are those dangers, and how pressing are they? Clearly, an unplanned pregnancy is one. Fortunately, there is some good news: Between 1990 and 2000, the teen pregnancy rate fell 36 percent (there was a corresponding drop in abortions and teen births as well).[44] The drop was due in part to teens delaying sex, but a bigger cause—86 percent of the decline, according to a Guttmacher Institute study—was the result of improved contraceptive use. In fact, the majority of sexually experienced teens (83 percent of girls and 91 percent of boys) say they used contraceptives the last time they had sex, up from 75 percent of girls and 82 percent of boys in 1995.[45]

Unfortunately, that trend may be reversing (although it's too soon to tell): In 2006, the teen birth rate rose 3 percent, the first time it has risen since 1991. And despite the overall drop in the past decade and a half, there are still far too many teen pregnancies. Today, about 1 million teens get pregnant each year, and 35 percent of young women get pregnant at least once before they reach the age of twenty.[46] Consider these statistics, too:

- Eighty-two percent of teen pregnancies are unplanned (compared to slightly more than half of all pregnancies).[47]
- More than half (57 percent) of teen pregnancies end in birth, 29 percent end in abortion, and 14 percent end in miscarriage.
- Eighteen- and nineteen-year-olds account for two-thirds of all teen pregnancies.[48]
- Eleven percent of all U.S. births are to teen mothers.[49]
- Teen mothers are now more likely than in the past to complete high school or obtain a GED, but they are still less likely than women who delay childbearing to go on to college.[50]
- The reasons teens most frequently give for having an abortion are concern about how having a baby would change their lives, inability to afford a baby, and feeling insufficiently mature to raise a child.[51]
- Thirty-four states (as of August 2006) require that a minor seeking an abortion involve her parents in the decision.[52]

FEARS AND REALITY: SEXUALLY TRANSMITTED INFECTIONS

Pregnancy isn't the only concern for sexually active teens. Sexually transmitted infections (STIs, a term that's increasingly used in place of sexually transmitted diseases or STDs) affect people of all ages, but as a group, teens make up the largest segment of new infections each year. In fact, although they only represent one-quarter of the population, young people in the United States (in this case, ages fifteen to twenty-four) make up nearly half of the 19 million new STI cases annually.[53]

In 2007, the U.S. Centers for Disease Control and Prevention (CDC) announced that a nationally representative study showed that one in four teenage girls has an STI, the most common of which was human papilloma virus (HPV). Teens also reported having trichomoniasis, chlamydia, and other STIs.

Among teens who acknowledged ever having had sex, the rate of STIs was 40 percent. That's a shocker for many parents, who likely underestimate how common STIs are, especially when it comes to their teen. Clearly, STIs are a risk. And while they may be more of a risk among certain groups—among African American girls in the CDC study the STI rate was 50 percent—STIs are found among all socioeconomic groups and ethnicities, which means your teen is not exempt, no matter how "nice" or "clean" or "smart" you think he is.

STI Primer

If it's been a while since you've thought about STIs, a refresher course might be in order. We'll explore the basics below. Both the CDC and the American Social Health Association (www.ashastd.org/learn/learn_statistics.cfm) offer a more in-depth look.

Human papilloma virus (HPV)

HPV infections are the most common STI reported in the United States and account for about half of the STIs diagnosed among fifteen- to twenty-four-year-olds each year. At some point in their lives, at least 50 percent of sexually active men and women will have an HPV infection; by age fifty, at least 80 percent of women will have had HPV.

HPV actually refers to a virus that has approximately a hundred different types, about forty of which are sexually transmitted. Some types of HPV cause genital warts, which are relatively harmless, but a few "high-risk" types can lead to cancer of the cervix, vulva, vagina, anus, or penis. HPV also may be linked to throat cancer.

Transmission and symptoms:
HPV is passed through genital contact, most often during vaginal or anal sex, but it can also be passed through oral sex. Infections often occur without symptoms, and a person can have it for years without knowing it.

Health problems:
If HPV doesn't go away on its own, it can lead to cervical and other cancers. HPV can also cause genital warts, although these are not linked to cancer.

Testing, treatment, and prevention:
Testing for HPV can be done from the same cells that are taken for a pap smear (the HPV test looks for the HPV virus, while the pap smear looks for changes in the cells of the cervix). There is no treatment for HPV, although there are treatments for the health problems it causes. Visible genital warts can be removed and cervical cell changes and cervical cancer can also be treated. Since HPV is passed by direct genital contact, condoms do offer some protection, but only in areas covered by a condom. A vaccination given to young women before they are exposed to HPV can protect them from the most common types of HPV (see page 80).

You might not know:
Cancers caused by HPV often show no symptoms until they're fairly advanced, which makes cancer screening—and HPV prevention—especially important.

Vaccinate for HPV

If you're a mom, you've probably had your share of pap smears and don't find them particularly controversial. For most women, they are a routine part of lifelong medical care. The reason you get a pap smear is to detect changes in your cervix that precede cervical cancer, which has been linked to HPV.

Despite this acceptance of the need for pap smears, the vaccine that protects against some types of HPV has been somewhat controversial—and the facts surrounding it sometimes distorted. The Centers for Disease Control and Prevention (CDC) now recommends that all girls between the ages of nine and twenty-three be given the vaccine, which is sold under the brand name Gardasil. HPV vaccines protect against the four HPV types that together cause 70 percent of cervical cancers and 90 percent of genital warts.

It's best for your teen to be vaccinated before she becomes sexually active (no matter how well you know her, there's no guarantee you'll know when she's going to have sex for the first time), since vaccines only protect against a virus you're not already infected with. The vaccine is also recommended for girls who are sexually active, since it's unlikely that a teen will already be infected with all four HPV types.

The vaccine is given in three injections over six months; it is thought to provide some protection after the second injection. Since it doesn't protect against all HPV strains, sexually active women should still have regular pap smears.

For now, it's not recommended boys be vaccinated, although its possible that vaccination could protect them from genital warts and some rare penile and anal cancers (and possible throat cancers) and obviously would help prevent them from infecting others. However, the HPV vaccine is being used for boys in Canada and Australia, and clinical trials are underway in the United States.

Chlamydia

Chlamydia is the most frequently reported bacterial STI in the United States. In fact, it may be even more common than documented because many cases fail to cause symptoms and therefore may go unnoticed.

Transmission and symptoms:

Chlamydia is transmitted by vaginal, anal, or oral sex. It causes no symptoms in three-quarters of infected women and half of infected men. When they are present, symptoms show up one to three weeks after infection. In women, they include abnormal vaginal discharge or a burning sensation when urinating; in men, a burning sensation or discharge from the penis. Symptoms of infection in the rectum (usually contracted by anal sex) can include rectal itching, burning, and bleeding.

Health problems:

If the disease spreads to the fallopian tubes, it can cause lower abdominal pain, low back pain, nausea, fever, pain during intercourse, or bleeding between menstrual periods. Untreated chlamydia can cause infertility and other health problems in girls as well as boys, although the data are not as good for boys.

Testing, treatment, and prevention:

The CDC recommends that all sexually active women under the age of twenty-five be screened for chlamydia at least once a year. Chlamydia can be treated and cured with antibiotics, and condoms reduce the risk of infection. There is also a urine screen for boys, and they should be tested once a year.

You might not know:
Teenage girls may be particularly at risk for contracting chlamydia because their cervixes are not fully matured and may be more prone to infection.[54] Women are often reinfected with chlamydia because their partners aren't treated. Men can also pass chlamydia to other men through anal or oral sex.

Trichomoniasis

Trichomoniasis is a common STI that affects both women and men but rarely gets much attention (the tricky-to-pronounce name doesn't help—it's trih-kuh-muh-nye-uh-sis). However, since it's the most common curable STI among young, sexually active women, it deserves greater awareness.

Transmission and symptoms:
The parasite that causes trichomoniasis is usually passed through vaginal intercourse, and the most common sites of infection are in the vagina for women and the urethra for men. Women can get it from men or women, but men usually only contract the infection from women.

Men often don't have symptoms, but when present, symptoms can include irritation inside the penis and a mild discharge or slight burning after urination or ejaculation. Symptoms in women include a frothy, yellow-green vaginal discharge with a strong odor and discomfort during intercourse and urination. Symptoms usually appear within five to twenty-eight days of exposure.

Health problems:
The inflammation trichomoniasis causes can increase a woman's risk of getting HIV if she's exposed. Having trichomoniasis can also increase the chance that an HIV-infected woman will pass HIV to her partner.

Testing, treatment, and prevention:
Testing is usually done by a physical examination (a doctor can detect visible signs in some women, although it's much harder in

men) and a lab test. Treatment usually involves a prescription drug taken by mouth in a single dose. Since a person can continue to reinfect a partner, it's important for both people to be treated at the same time. Condoms can reduce the risk of infection.

You might not know:
Symptoms might not exist for a man or might disappear on their own, but an infected man can continue to reinfect a female partner if he hasn't been treated.

Risky Business

All sexual contact carries some risk. Certain STIs (including herpes, syphilis, and HPV, to name three) can be transmitted even when a condom is used.

Of course, some types of contact are riskier than others. Unprotected anal sex is particularly risky for the transmission of HIV and other STIs because the lining of the anus is thin and poorly lubricated and therefore breaks more easily than the lining of the vagina. Those breaks allow an entry point for STIs.

But any cuts, sores, or skin breaks—a cold sore, a small cut in your gum, irritation in the skin of the vagina or penis—can allow for transmission of infections, so oral and vaginal sex also carry risks. (And remember, other STIs can be transmitted simply through genital contact—no breaks needed.)

The bottom line: There's no such thing as risk-free sex. Unprotected sex clearly is most risky, with unprotected anal sex topping the chart of behaviors high in risk for transmitting HIV and other STIs. Your teen needs to reduce exposure as much as possible by limiting his number of sexual partners, choosing partners carefully to avoid those who have risk factors themselves, and always using a condom.

Syphilis

Syphilis is a bacterial infection that has been on the rise in recent years. Most cases occur in the twenty- to thirty-nine-year-old age group. And while 64 percent occur in men who have sex with men, syphilis can affect sexually active people of any age or orientation.

Transmission and symptoms: Syphilis is transmitted by direct contact with syphilis sores, which mainly affect the external genitals, vagina, anus, or rectum, but can also occur on the mouth. You can't catch syphilis by touching a doorknob, sitting on a toilet seat, or through other casual contact.

Most people don't show symptoms for years and are unaware they're infected. During the primary phase, symptoms include a sore (called a chancre) or sores, which are usually firm, round, and painless. They most often occur on the genitals, although they can show up on the anus, mouth, fingers, and breasts. Chancres last for three to six weeks and heal on their own. But if there's no treatment (which is necessary even if the chancres heal on their own), the disease progresses to the secondary stage, which includes a skin rash that usually appears on the palms of the hands or bottoms of the feet (although it can occur anywhere). Sometimes the rash is so minimal it's not noticed. Other symptoms include fever, swollen lymph glands, sore throat, patchy hair loss, headaches, weight loss, muscle aches, and fatigue. Symptoms go away on their own, but the disease progresses to the latent stage and can progress after many years to the late stage, which can lead to damage to the internal organs, bones, and joints.

Health problems:
Syphilis can be deadly to a developing baby, so pregnant women should be tested. If left untreated and allowed to develop to the late stage, syphilis can result in blindness, dementia, mobility problems, paralysis, and even death.

Testing, treatment, and prevention:
Diagnosis is either determined visually based on the chancre or through a blood test. During the early stages, syphilis is easily

cured with antibiotics. Condoms can provide some protection, although they don't protect the areas they don't cover.

You might not know:
Chancres and open sores from other STIs make it easier to transmit and acquire HIV.

Gonorrhea
Gonorrhea is a common bacterial STI that, after years of decline, is on the rise again. It can affect any sexually active person, but the highest rates of infection are among teens, young adults, and African Americans.

Transmission and symptoms:
Gonorrhea is spread through contact with the genitals, the mouth, or the anus. Most women show no signs of being infected, although some report symptoms such as a burning sensation when urinating, increased vaginal discharge, or bleeding between periods. Some men also have no symptoms, although some report a burning sensation when urinating; a white, yellow, or green discharge from the penis; and painful or swollen testicles. Rectal infection can cause no symptoms, but it can also cause discharge, anal itching, soreness, bleeding, or painful bowel movements in both men and women. Infections in the throat usually have no symptoms.

Health problems:
In women, gonorrhea can cause pelvic inflammatory disease (see page 87) and problems in pregnancy. In men it can cause infertility, and in both sexes it can spread to the blood or joints, which can be life threatening.

Testing, treatment, and prevention:
Gonorrhea can be detected through a urine test or other tests. It can usually be treated with antibiotics, but drug-resistant strains are becoming increasingly common. Condoms can protect against gonorrhea.

You might not know:
Having gonorrhea makes a person more likely to acquire HIV if exposed, and it makes HIV-positive people more infectious.

Genital Herpes
Genital herpes can be caused by either of two herpes simplex viruses: type 1 or type 2, although most cases are type 2. Type 1 more often causes "fever blisters," sores that appear on the lips and mouth. In the United States today, genital herpes infections are on the decline, but the virus still affects at least 45 million people.

Transmission and symptoms:
Genital herpes is passed by contact with the genitals of an infected person and can be passed even when an infected person has no visible signs of infection. Most people have only minor symptoms or no symptoms and don't know they're infected. When symptoms do occur for the first time, it's usually about two weeks after infection. Typically, the outbreak is in the form of blisters on or around the genitals or anus (the blisters then break and leave sores that take two to four weeks to heal), although secondary symptoms of the first outbreak can include flu-like symptoms and fever. An infected person might have several outbreaks in the first year of infection and then fewer infections after the first year. Subsequent outbreaks are usually less severe and shorter, although the virus is still present.

Health problems:
Herpes outbreaks can be painful. In addition, since it's not curable and there's a social stigma associated with herpes, simply having the virus is often distressing. Herpes also may make people more susceptible to HIV infection if they're exposed to it, and it can make HIV-infected people more infectious.

Testing, treatment, and prevention:
Herpes is usually diagnosed based on visible symptoms, although there is a blood test that can detect the virus. Although there is no cure, medications can help lessen symptoms and decrease the likelihood of giving it to partners.

You might not know:
It's easier for the virus to pass from males to females. Therefore, more women have the virus than men do.

Pelvic Inflammatory Disease (PID)

PID is not an STI, per se, but a complication of STIs that occurs when an infection reaches the uterus, fallopian tubes, or other reproductive organs. It typically occurs when STIs (most commonly chlamydia and gonorrhea) go untreated, and it can lead to permanent damage of the reproductive organs or other serious complications.

Transmission and symptoms:
PID sometimes causes no symptoms; when they do occur, symptoms can range from mild to severe. The most common are lower abdominal pain, fever, unusual vaginal discharge that may have a foul odor, painful intercourse, painful urination, and irregular menstrual bleeding.

Women who douche are more likely to suffer from PID, and the more sex partners a woman has, the greater her likelihood of having PID. Having a partner who has multiple sex partners can also increase a woman's risk, because she'll likely be exposed to more STIs.

Health problems:
PID can cause inflammation and scarring of the fallopian tubes, leading to infertility and the potential for ectopic pregnancies, and other reproductive organs. It can also cause chronic pelvic pain.

Testing, treatment, and prevention:

If there are no symptoms, or symptoms are mild, PID often goes undiagnosed until a person experiences infertility or an ectopic pregnancy. However, a lab test for STIs can clue a health provider in to the possibility of PID, and an ultrasound can help identify any effects on the reproductive organs. If caught early, permanent damage can be minimized. PID is often treated with antibiotics, which target the infection that caused PID. However, such treatment won't reverse any damage that has already been done. Condoms can reduce the risk of contracting certain STIs, and annual testing for chlamydia can help identify an infection so it can be treated.

In addition, it's important for women to hear the message that STIs can do serious damage if they're left untreated. Therefore, women should reduce their risk but also take charge of their reproductive health care, which boils down to this: Get tested if your sexual activity warrants testing, and get treatment if you suspect you have an STI.

You might not know:

PID affects greater numbers of young women, probably because young women are more likely to be exposed to STIs, and their not fully matured cervixes are more likely to allow an infection to progress through the reproductive system.

Human Immunodeficiency Virus (HIV)

HIV is the virus that causes AIDS (acquired immunodeficiency syndrome) and is the most deadly of sexually transmitted infections. It is incurable, although advances in treatment in the past fifteen years have made it a disease that can often be kept under control for years. Still, although treatment can prolong life, it is often costly and difficult.

In the United States, HIV infections have dropped noticeably from 150,000 a year in the early 1980s to about 40,000 new infections per year today.

Before you breathe a sigh of relief, though, consider this: Young people (under twenty-four) account for roughly 50 percent of those infections. In addition, about one-quarter of the 1 million people living with HIV or AIDS don't know they're infected, which means they may unknowingly put others at risk.[55] While HIV was once thought of as a disease that only infected drug users and gay men, today women account for one-quarter of all new HIV infections. High-risk heterosexual contact—including unprotected vaginal, anal, or oral sex—accounts for about 80 percent of those cases.

There are many misperceptions about HIV, so we'll give a quick refresher course on the basics. First, the virus is primarily found in the blood, semen, and vaginal fluid of an infected person, which means you can only get it by being exposed to those fluids (in other words, you can't get it by shaking hands, sharing utensils, hugging, or having other casual contact with an HIV-infected person). HIV is mainly passed in three ways: through sexual contact, by sharing needles with an infected person, and from mother to child through childbirth or breastfeeding—clearly a problem in poor countries.

Assuming that you don't know the HIV status of a partner, the most common behaviors that put a person at risk for contracting HIV are: injecting drugs with shared needles; having unprotected sex with men who have sex with men, multiple partners, or anonymous partners; having received a blood transfusion between 1978 and 1985; and having unprotected sex with someone who has any of these risk factors.

Sexual behaviors do vary in risk. Some examples, from most to least risky:

- receptive anal intercourse
- receptive vaginal intercourse
- insertive anal intercourse
- insertive vaginal intercourse
- receptive oral sex
- insertive oral sex

Generally, male-to-female or male-to-male transmission is more likely than female-to-male or female-to-female.

Having another STI is also a risk factor. People who have an STI are two to five times more likely to acquire HIV infection if they're exposed to the virus through sexual contact. This is because many STIs cause open sores or small lesions through which the virus can more easily pass into the bloodstream. Similarly, people infected with HIV who are also infected with another STI are more likely to transmit HIV through sexual contact than are HIV-positive people who don't have other STIs.

Most people who are infected with HIV don't have symptoms for many years, so it's possible to be infected—and infectious—without showing any outward signs. In addition, most HIV tests actually look for antibodies in a person's bloodstream rather than the virus itself, and since it can take up to three months for the body to develop antibodies, there can be a lag before an infected person will actually test positive for HIV. Tests that look for the virus can be taken within three weeks of being infected, although they're not as widely available.

The good news is that condoms can provide protection from the virus. Teens have been on the receiving end of education efforts about HIV for years (89 percent have been taught about it in school),[56] which means many are well versed in the topic, and some even view getting an HIV test as the responsible thing to do, whether or not they have risk factors. At the same time, quicker and easier HIV testing is now widely available.

Still, there is recent evidence that young people—and, in particular, men who have sex with other men, whose rates of infection are once again on the rise—have become less vigilant about HIV prevention in recent years, thanks in part to improved treatments that make HIV more of a chronic, manageable disease than it once was. The potential for a false sense of security means it's especially important for parents to talk to their teens about avoiding high-risk sexual behaviors, reducing the number of partners they have, and consistently using condoms.

SAFER SEX

In all that's changed since you were a teen, one thing has stayed the same: abstinence, or not having sex, is the best way to avoid pregnancy and STIs. In a survey by the National Campaign to Prevent Teen Pregnancy, parents and teens alike said it's a valid and worthy message for teens to hear.[57] In fact, teens said they want more information about abstinence. But they also said they value information about birth control and condoms so that they can make informed decisions if they do decide to have sex.

If you're reading this book, chances are your teen hasn't abstained, at least on one occasion. And even if your teen decides that being sexually active isn't the right choice for now, it's important to get the message across that every sexually active teen needs to be responsible for reducing risk by limiting her number of sexual partners, avoiding high-risk activities, and practicing safer sex (just so you know, the term "safe sex" is still used, but safer sex, or protected sex, is preferred because no sex is entirely without risk).

One way to have safer sex is to use birth control and to have just one monogamous partner who is known to be STI-free. Birth control, when consistently and properly used, can be a highly effective way of avoiding an unintended pregnancy. And if both partners are STI-free and neither has sex with anyone else or participates in other risky behavior—such as injecting drugs with shared needles—sex is pretty safe as far as infections go. Of course, this assumes that you know the other person's status with certainty, which is hardly a given, even if the partner has been tested for STIs. Not all STIs are routinely tested for, and some tests, including the one for HIV, won't identify recent infections. Therefore, if you don't know with absolute certainty that your partner is STI-free, STIs are a risk. In that case, safer sex means using a condom (throw in a back-up birth-control method for even safer sex in terms of pregnancy prevention).

Condom Use Is Up

Fortunately, condoms have some strong selling points: They are relatively inexpensive and easy to get, fairly easy to use (with some practice), and when used properly, very effective in preventing the exchange of bodily fluids.

And teens *are* using condoms more than their counterparts did a decade and a half ago. In fact, of sexually active high schoolers, 63 percent say they or their partner wore a condom the last time they had intercourse. That's a notable increase from 1991, when 46.2 percent of teens used condoms.[58]

Unfortunately, those gains seem to be slowing. Condom use has leveled off since 2003, possibly due to an upswing in abstinence-only education that limits discussion of condoms and focuses on birth control and condom failure rates. In addition, the current level of use still means 37 percent of teens are having sex without a condom, a far higher number than is reported in many other developed countries.

It's also important to note that condoms aren't foolproof—they sometimes break and can be used incorrectly (with perfect use, for example, they're 98 percent effective in preventing pregnancy, but with typical use they're only 85 percent effective). Some people also complain that they are uncomfortable or say they reduce pleasure. In addition, as good as they are at preventing the exchange of fluids, condoms don't protect the areas they don't cover, including the scrotum, vulva, and anus, leaving room for STIs to spread even when a condom is used. And although teen condom use during vaginal intercourse has improved, condoms still aren't regularly used during oral and anal sex.

Are All Condoms Equal?

Condoms coated with spermicide might seem like a good idea (pregnancy prevention and STI protection all in one, right?), but the American Social Health Association and the World Health Organization (WHO) now recommend against their use. The reason: Condoms lubricated with spermicide don't significantly reduce the likelihood of pregnancy and can cause skin irritation, which can increase a person's likelihood of getting HIV if exposed. Of course, WHO points out that it's better to use a condom with spermicide than no condom at all.

Condoms of any kind also require proper use to be effective. The American Social Health Association has tips on condom use on its teen website (www. iwannaknow.org) and an animated sequence showing proper condom use at (www.ashastd.org/condom/condom_introduction.cfm).

In addition to knowing how to use one, all teens should know that condoms can be damaged by:

- oil-based lubricants (such as baby oil, Vaseline, or hand cream)
- age (check the best-used-by date and toss any that are past their prime)
- heat
- sunlight
- humidity
- "doubling up," or using two condoms (doubled-up condoms tend to break)

Finally, novelty condoms may not offer protection against pregnancy or STIs. Read the label to be sure.

Don't Forget the Dam

If you're a bit fuzzy on the concept of a dental dam, you're not alone. Apart from the dentist's office—where one type of dental dam is used to cover a person's mouth during dental work—dams don't get much lip service, much less use. They are, it seems, the forgotten piece of the STI-prevention puzzle.

So why does the dam get no respect? It's hard to say, but it may be that as risky behaviors go, people—and teens in particular—view oral sex as fairly low on the danger totem pole. And while that perception may be on target (the chance of passing HIV via unprotected oral sex is far lower than the risk of passing it via unprotected anal sex, for example), STIs—including herpes, HPV, chlamydia, and other infections—can be passed via oral sex. Condoms should be worn for oral sex performed on a man (fellatio) and dams should be used when engaging in vaginal oral sex (cunnilingus). In addition, a dam should always be used during any oral-anal contact (anilingus).

Depending on what type of sex education he's getting and what type of information he's finding on his own, your teen might never have heard of a dam, which means it's up to you to spread the good word. Here's what you should know (and tell your teen) about dams:

- Dams are latex or polyurethane sheets that are available at some pharmacies and online.
- To use a dam, you spread it over the person's vagina or anus during oral sex. The dam acts as a barrier to prevent the exchange of fluids or direct contact between the mouth and genitals or anus.
- Before using a dental dam, you should check it for holes by holding it up to the light.
- You can use a water-based personal lubricant to enhance sensation and keep the dam in place (but don't use baby oil or other oils because they can damage latex).
- You should only use a dental dam once.
- In a pinch, a condom can be used (slice it down the middle, open it and spread it over the vagina), as can plastic wrap (although neither method is as effective as a real dental dam because both are susceptible to tearing).

PILLS, PATCHES, AND SHOTS, OH MY

Although science may one day develop a handy solution, for now the only birth control options for boys and men are condoms and vasectomy—a surgical procedure that permanently sterilizes males and isn't a reasonable option for most teen boys. Thus, beyond condom use, the responsibility for birth control often falls to females. Fortunately, there are plenty of options for teens to choose from.

One of the best known is the birth control pill (aka "the pill," or oral contraceptives). About 16 percent of sexually active teens say they or their partner use birth control pills to prevent pregnancy, and a quarter of those say they use both condoms and birth control pills.

The pill works by releasing the hormones estrogen and progestin, which prevent a woman's ovaries from releasing eggs. It is highly effective but must be taken every day, at roughly the same time of day—a requirement that may be daunting for some teens.

In addition, some antibiotics and other medications reduce the effectiveness of the pill, and there can be side effects, such as bleeding between periods, breast tenderness, nausea, and vomiting. People who smoke or have diabetes or certain other conditions may be at increased risk of some of the more severe side effects, including heart attack, stroke, blood clots, and high blood pressure. Finally, it's important to note that the pill does not protect at all against STIs, so the 25 percent that use both condoms and birth control pills have the right idea (and ought to be joined by the other 75 percent).

In addition to preventing pregnancy, all hormonal birth control methods (we'll go over the rest in a moment) have some added bonuses for some women: They can result in lighter or more regular periods, reduced menstrual cramps, reduced acne, and fewer symptoms associated with premenstrual syndrome (PMS). For this reason some teens will ask to go on the pill even if they're not having sex.

Some of the other hormonal options, which work in much the same way as the pill (and have many of the same pros and cons), are:

- **Birth control patch**—A thin beige plastic patch that's worn on the skin like a bandage and changed weekly. It prevents pregnancy by releasing estrogen and progestin, is low maintenance (the user only has to apply it once a week), and is very effective when used properly. One downside is that it's visible, although it can be worn discreetly.
- **Depo-Provera**—An injection of hormones that lasts three months. It's probably the most effective of the hormonal methods because it requires no intervention from the user. But the fact that it involves a shot puts off some teens.
- **Nuva Ring**—A small, flexible ring that's inserted into the vagina, left in place for three weeks, and then removed and replaced a week later with a new ring. It releases estrogen and progestin and is highly effective when used properly. However, it does involve touching the genitals, so young teens may find it off-putting. In addition, it can cause vaginal irritation (in 1 to 2.5 percent of women), which, in theory, could lead to a greater likelihood of contracting some STIs when exposed to them.
- **Implant**—Implanon is an approved but not yet widely available flexible piece of plastic that is inserted under the skin of the upper arm and releases progestin, thereby preventing the ovaries from releasing eggs. It is highly effective, low-maintenance (you don't have to "do" anything for it to work), and lasts for about three years, although some people may feel uncomfortable with the concept of having something implanted under their skin.

Women also have a choice of birth control methods that don't rely on hormones to prevent pregnancy. Those options include:

- **The female condom**—A long, plastic pouch with flexible rings on either end, the female condom is inserted into the vagina before intercourse and removed immediately after. On the upside, it's easy to obtain and convenient if you need it only occasionally (if you're only having sex infrequently, for example), and it removes any objections by a male based on "fit" (unlike a male condom, it doesn't require a snug fit). It also provides protection from some STIs (although it doesn't protect the areas it doesn't cover) and has fewer potential side effects than the hormonal methods. But it does involve touching their own genitals, so young teens may not be as comfortable using it or may find it hard to use.

- **IUDs**—Intrauterine devices are small, flexible plastic devices that are inserted into the uterus by a clinician. (One, Mirena, releases a small amount of the hormone levonorgestrel directly into the uterus.) They are highly effective, long lasting, low maintenance, and discreet, and when removed offer a quick return to fertility. However, IUDs don't protect against STIs.

- **Spermicides**—Spermicides come in creams, foams, jellies, and suppositories. They immobilize sperm to prevent them from reaching the uterus. The most common active ingredient is nonoxynol 9. When used according to package directions, spermicides are 85 percent effective. They're especially useful for people who have sex infrequently, although some people complain that they're messy or cause irritation. In addition, they don't protect against STIs (despite some misperceptions that they protect against HIV, in particular) and frequent use in some women might cause irritation that actually increases the risk of contracting HIV if exposed. Since such irritation can occur without symptoms, the Food and Drug Administration recommends the use of spermicides without a condom only for people who are in a monogamous relationship with a partner who is known to be HIV-free and who has no other sexual partners or HIV risk factors. If you can't be certain that you meet those criteria, we recommend using another method.

- **The contraceptive sponge**—The Today Sponge, approved for sale in the United States (other brands are available outside the United States and via the Internet), is inserted into the vagina before intercourse and prevents sperm from reaching the cervix. It also contains a spermicide and does not protect against STIs.
- **Diaphragms, shields, and cups**—These are silicone barriers that cover a woman's cervix and prevent sperm from reaching the uterus. They must be provided by a health care professional and are effective, but they require some practice in proper use. They do not protect against STIs.
- **Fertility awareness**—This involves carefully tracking your fertility—by noting your temperature and/or cervical mucus and/or menstrual history (rhythm method)—and then refraining from sex on the days that conception is most likely. This may be too complicated and time-consuming for most teens to practice accurately. It also offers no protection against STIs.
- **Withdrawal**—Using this method, the man withdraws his penis from the vagina before he ejaculates. In typical use, it is about 83 percent effective, but it's not recommended for teens because it provides no protection against STIs and requires more control than many sexually inexperienced males have. In addition, there is a small amount of sperm in pre-ejaculate—the fluid that is released before ejaculation—which means it's slightly risky even when done correctly.

Your teen's doctor can talk in detail about which option is best for her. Considerations may include how safe and effective it will be, how well it fits into her lifestyle and future plans, affordability, and convenience.

Birth Control Laws

In most states, teens who want access to birth control can get it, with or without their parents' involvement or notification. In fact, twenty-one states and the District of Columbia explicitly say that teens (usually over the age of fourteen) can get contraceptives without a parent's involvement, and twenty-five states allow for teen consent under certain circumstances, according to the Guttmacher Institute.

Teens across the nation also have the right to consent to testing and treatment for STIs without parental permission (although some states allow for a parent to be notified if a doctor feels it's in the best interests of the minor). Thirty-one states include HIV treatment and testing in their definition of health services teens can consent to.

When it comes to abortion, access is far more restricted. In fact, thirty-five states require parental involvement (either parental permission or simply notification) for teens under the age of eighteen.

Emergency Contraception

Sometimes dubbed the "morning-after pill"—despite the fact that it's actually more than one pill and can be taken later than the "morning after"—Plan B is the brand name for emergency contraception (plan A refers to not getting pregnant in the first place). It can be taken up to five days after unprotected sex, although it's most effective if taken within twenty-four hours and is often used in cases of sexual assault, when a condom breaks or other birth control fails, or when no protection was used.

Plan B contains the hormone progestin—the same hormone that's in regular birth control pills (most regular birth control pills also have estrogen), but at a higher dose—and can reduce the risk of pregnancy by 89 percent. Typically, it is taken in two doses: one pill within 72 hours of intercourse and a second pill 12 hours later. It works by preventing the ovaries from releasing an egg or preventing an egg from being fertilized or attaching to the uterus wall. It's not the same as the so-called "abortion pill," which ends a pregnancy after an egg has been fertilized.

Emergency contraception is now available over the counter to anyone over the age of eighteen, but it's helpful for all teens to know that women may be able to use their own birth control pills as emergency contraception by taking a higher dose immediately after intercourse. Since pills vary in dosage and type, it's best to ask your teen's doctor to talk to her about if and how she can use her pills in the event that she has unprotected sex. It's also a good idea for a sexually active teen to ask her doctor about emergency contraception even if she's not taking birth control pills. (If you're wondering why a teen with birth control pills would need emergency contraception, keep in mind the teen might have skipped a dose or discontined her prescription.) You can also get information about emergency contraception (or direct your teen to get information for herself) at www.not-2-late.com (developed by Princeton University and the Association of Repro-ductive Health Professionals). More information about emergency contraception is also available at the National Women's Health Information Center, www.4woman.gov/FAQ/birthcont.htm, oper-ated by the federal government.

Bear in mind that emergency contraceptives in pill form only prevent pregnancy in 75 to 89 percent of cases (depending on the type of emergency contraceptive used and when it's used). More effective as emergency contraception is an IUD, which must be inserted by a doctor within five days of unprotected sex but is 99 percent effective in preventing pregnancy. This might be a good option for someone who had unprotected sex and wanted an IUD for future birth control anyway, or for someone who had unprotected sex during the most fertile period of her reproductive cycle and for whom a 75 percent success rate is unacceptable. However, since it prevents implantation of a fertil-ized egg, some people might object to it on moral grounds.

SEEING A DOCTOR

If your teen has had sex and hasn't already talked to a doctor about being sexually active, now's the time. Even for teens who feel up to snuff on the basics—or who've already had a first gynecological visit—it's important to see a doctor because becoming sexually active has potential health implications. A doctor can screen for STIs, talk to your teen about birth control and avoiding risky sex, and answer any questions that pertain specifically to your teen.

This is especially important for boys, who often aren't as hooked in to the health care system and might miss out on reproductive health care or STI screenings. And teens of both sexes may tell a doctor things they'd never feel comfortable telling a parent. So, if you've just found out your teen is sexually active, you'll want to suggest making an appointment as soon as possible.

Your first instinct may be to head to your pediatrician's office, and it's not a bad idea. After all, your teen will be in familiar territory and may be more likely to open up to someone who is already a known entity, especially if the two have a good relationship. But not all doctors are geared toward, or good at, working with teens. Therefore, you might consider making an appointment with an adolescent medicine specialist—a doctor trained to care for teens—or a gynecologist who specializes in treating young women.

If you decide she should see the pediatrician first, call the doctor's office to find out how they handle such visits. Does your teen's pediatrician feel comfortable talking to teens about sex, birth control, and STIs? Not all do. Is there another doctor in the practice who is more experienced and comfortable with teens? You should also ask whether the pediatrician can test for STIs and prescribe birth control or whether you'll be referred to another doctor, such as a gynecologist (in which case you might want to go right to the gynecologist and save the pediatrician's talk for the next scheduled visit). Finally, ask whether the pediatrician makes accommodations—such as longer appointments—for teens visiting for reproductive health issues, especially for the first visit, which can take longer than a typical well-child checkup.

If you're planning to take your teenage daughter to a gynecologist, your own doctor may be a good option, but do a little homework here, too. Does your gynecologist regularly treat teens? Or is there a gynecologist trained in treating adolescents nearby? Such doctors typically have smaller instruments that are more comfortable for teens and are geared to handle teens' needs. Your teen's wishes are also important. Does she feel comfortable seeing her mother's doctor? Some teens would rather start fresh with a new doctor.

Your options may be limited by insurance, but ideally you'll find a doctor who can and will take the necessary time to talk to your teen about sex, find out what medical concerns your teen might have, and then address them appropriately.

What Her Doctor Looks For

When it's time for your teen's visit, her doctor may speak to you both to get a personal and family medical history. But after that, the doctor will almost certainly ask to speak to your teen alone. That's ideal, because full disclosure on the part of your teen is critical to effective medical care, and she may feel embarrassed or afraid to talk freely if you're present.

When the doctor is alone with your teen, he or she will probably spend a little time trying to get to know her. Many adolescent medicine doctors strive to follow the mnemonic SSHADESS (or a variation of it) as they talk to and evaluate a teen patient. SSHADESS[59] stands for:

Strengths
School
Home
Activities
Drugs and other substances
Emotions
Sexuality
Safety

In going through the SSHADESS routine, a doctor might ask
your teen:

- **What she sees as her strengths**—Is she creative? Organized? Outgoing? Intelligent? How does she see herself?
- **How things are at school**—What kind of grades does she
  get? Does she struggle academically or find it a breeze? Is
  her social network at school or elsewhere? What other
  school-related activities is she involved in?
- **How things are at home**—Who does she live with? What is
  her relationship with parents and siblings? Have there been
  any major changes in family life recently? Does she feel generally happy at home?
- **What she does in her spare time**—What are her hobbies or
  pursuits? What does she do on the weekends? With whom
  does she spend most of her time?
- **Whether she uses drugs or alcohol**—If she does, how
  often? In what context? Does she engage in risky behaviors
  when she's under the influence?
- **Her overall health**—Is she sleeping well? Eating well? Feeling generally healthy?
- **Her emotional health**—Is she generally happy? Does she
  feel stressed or upset often? Is she depressed?
- **What her plans are for the future**—Does she plan to go to
  college? To pursue a particular career path? To get married?
  To have children?
- **Whether she's in a relationship**—How long has she been
  in it? Who is she dating?
- **Whether she's sexually active**—How long has she been
  sexually active? How often does she have sex? What kind of
  sexual activity is she engaged in? When was the last time she
  had sex?
- **Her level of sexual risk**—How many partners has she had?
  Has she had unprotected sex and, if so, how often? Is she
  using birth control? Does she have any symptoms she's concerned about? Does she have any other concerns related to

sexual activity or safety? Does sexual activity occur while she's drunk or high and, if so, how often? Has she had unprotected sex with any partners who might fall into a high-risk group?

TESTS AND EXAMINATIONS

Once the doctor has gotten to know your teen, she'll likely talk to her about birth control and STI protection. Depending on your teen's answers to the above, she may or may not order tests. Tests that may be recommended are:

- a urine test for pregnancy
- a culture for gonorrhea or chlamydia
- a blood test for HIV or syphilis (generally doctors do this only if a teen has had four or more partners or has a partner who has had multiple partners, although they may recommend a test if they suspect other risk factors)
- a blood test to diagnose herpes if there is concern that she has contracted it. However, if lesions are visible, the doctor might clinically diagnose herpes without a test.

Of course, teens may request certain tests, and doctors often will oblige. Some teens like to know that they're HIV-free or free of other STIs, even if they're not particularly at risk.

Depending on your teen's age, her doctor may also recommend a pap smear to test for cervical cancer (which is linked to HPV, a sexually transmitted infection). But don't be surprised if the doctor forgoes a pap smear. Recent protocols recommend that pap smears begin three years after a woman's sexual debut. So if a teen first has sex at fifteen, she won't need a pap smear until she's eighteen.

If your teen hasn't passed the three-year mark, her doctor probably also won't do a pelvic exam, unless there is a specific reason to do one. However, she will examine her abdomen externally (to check for tenderness that might be a sign of pelvic inflammatory disease or other problems) and check the external genitalia to screen for signs of sexual abuse or STIs.

If your teen hasn't already been vaccinated for HPV, your doctor will likely recommend she start the vaccination series now. It won't protect her from any HPV types she's already contracted, but it can protect against types she hasn't contracted.

If your teen is a boy, the discussion will center on the same types of issues, although his doctor will also discuss penile care. For uncircumcised boys and men, retracting the foreskin and cleaning underneath helps reduce the risk of infection, a fact your teen's doctor will likely address.

Finally, the doctor will talk to your teen about what he or she feels comfortable revealing to the parent. The teen is the patient, so except in certain circumstances—if the doctor believes your teen is in immediate danger, for example—she'll only report back to you with your teen's permission. Before your teen leaves, the doctor will likely ask how she would like to receive the results to any tests that are done. Your teen may opt to retrieve test results personally or tell the doctor's office not to call your home phone number with results.

Finding a Doctor

Getting referrals from people who are happy with their own doctor is a great way to find a good doctor. But you can also check with your local hospital, which may have a referral service or search feature on its website, or with professional organizations that allow you to search for a doctor by specialty and location.

Some options:

American Academy of Pediatrics: www.aap.org

American College of Obstetrics and Gynecology: www.acog.org

American Social Health Association: www.ashastd.org; for the STI resource center hotline (which can provide referrals) call 919.361.8488, and for pre-recorded STI information call 800.227.8922.

American Urological Association: www.urologyhealth. org (for boys and men)

HIVtest.org: www.hivtest.org (to find local testing centers)

National Family Planning and Reproductive Health Association: www.nfprha.org

Planned Parenthood Federation of America: www.plannedparenthood.org (offers reproductive health services for both sexes)

Society for Adolescent Medicine: www.adolescenthealth.org (includes doctors in a variety of disciplines)

TEEN PREGNANCY: WHEN A TEST IS POSITIVE

You're standing in your kitchen reeling from shock: Your sixteen-year-old teen has just dropped a bomb—she thinks she's pregnant. Last week you were talking SATs, homecoming dresses, and college-prep courses. And suddenly the future seems, well, scary. Will she finish high school? Go to college? If she has a baby, who will raise it? Of all the hopes and dreams you had for her, getting pregnant while she's still in high school wasn't one of them.

If your teen is holding the end of a pregnancy test wand and staring in disbelief at the little pink plus sign, she may be feeling a range of emotions: fear, sadness, disappointment, shame, resolve, happiness, excitement, or a combination.

Her biggest initial fear might not be the concept of having a baby (she may not have gotten her arms around that one yet) but rather the fear of telling you, her parent. You have, after all, likely given her the message that a teen pregnancy isn't in your plan for her. And even if you've been open, honest, forgiving, and nonjudgmental, she may fear disappointing you.

Her concern may be well founded. You might be disappointed, angry, or sad. Or maybe not. Either way, it's important to focus on your teen's emotions and needs, rather than your own. This is, after all, primarily *her* challenge. Your job will be to make sure that she has the resources to make the best decision for her present and future well-being, as well as the well-being of a child, if she chooses to have the baby.

Positive Response

If your teen comes to you to report that she's pregnant (we'll get to teenage boys in a moment), there are steps you can take to make sure your response is a healthy one:

- **Collect yourself.** Breaking down in sobs and dire predictions of a life ruined isn't going to help, and it may well do some serious damage. If you need a moment, acknowledge that you're shocked (surprised, stunned, whatever) and ask for a moment to collect yourself. Your goal now should be to get those emotions in check; you can explore them later, after her immediate needs are met.
- **Separate your own experience from hers.** If you have strong feelings about teen sex, teen pregnancy, abortion, adoption, or teen parenting, you may need to separate your own values from your teen's. Remember, you can't dictate values. She'll need to make her own decision and live with it, so it's important that you give her room to do so.
- **Get a read on your teen's emotions.** She may be in full panic mode, distraught, upset, and crying. Or she may be

perfectly calm, having had a little more time than you to adjust to the news. Take a moment to assess her and deter- mine how much emotional support she needs from you right now. And consider her emotions going forward. In the days to come, she may feel guilt, shame, depression, sadness, like a failure, or overwhelmed at the decisions she must make. Keep her emotional health in mind and offer support if she needs it.

- **Tell her you love her.** One of her biggest fears most likely is that her announcement will cause you to love or respect her less. Even if you're angry, and even if you think she knows you love her, take a moment to point out that, regardless of the situation, your love is unchanged. And give her a hug— she could probably use one right about now.

- **Get more information.** Find out why your teen thinks she's pregnant. When did she last menstruate and for how long? Did she take an over-the-counter urine test? Is she guessing based on symptoms? If she had a positive result from a home pregnancy test, you should seek to confirm it, either with a second test, or better, by visiting the doctor.

- **Get a medical opinion.** Call your teen's pediatrician, gyne- cologist, or an adolescent medicine doctor, explain the situa- tion, and ask for the next steps. Her doctor will likely want to see her immediately to confirm the pregnancy, determine how far along she is, and talk to her about her options. Early medi- cal care is important regardless of what your teen ultimately decides to do. If the pregnancy continues, early prenatal care can give it the best chance of success; if she decides to ter- minate, it will be easier earlier in the pregnancy than later.

- **Remind her about precautions.** Until she gets to the doctor to confirm the pregnancy, your teen should refrain from smok- ing, drugs, and alcohol. You can also remind her to have her partner wear a condom for STI protection.

- **Talk about the father.** She may have already told the baby's father. Or not. Find out and then talk to her about how much or little she wants to involve him and what her expectations are about his involvement.

Three Options for Pregnant Teens

You may want to wait until the pregnancy is confirmed and your teen has talked to a doctor before talking to her yourself about options. Realistically, though, it may be hard not to think (and talk) about what she is going to do.

If you do launch right into that discussion, you can outline three choices. She can:

- Have the baby and raise it herself (or with help from you, her partner, or someone else)
- Have the baby and give it up for adoption
- Have an abortion to terminate the pregnancy

The realities surrounding each of the options have changed dramatically in the past twenty years, so your perception of each may be out of date. First, the social stigma associated with being a teen parent has faded considerably, and support offerings have grown so that many teen parents are able to finish high school and go on to college and/or successful careers. Similarly, the stigma surrounding adoption has also diminished, and to a lesser degree (depending on your community) so too has the stigma surrounding abortion. Adoption methods have also changed. Open adoptions, in which the birth mother may have contact with the child throughout childhood, are now the norm, because much of the secrecy and shame surrounding adoption has been pushed aside.

A full exploration of everything that will go into a pregnant teen's choices is beyond the scope of this book, but in general the major considerations are:

- How her choice will affect her future plans for high school, college, and beyond
- Whether she can afford to have and raise a baby
- Whether the father of the baby will be involved and how much support he can be expected to offer

- How she feels emotionally about each option, or whether any of the choices violate her beliefs or values
- How she feels about her ability to handle the challenges of each option
- Whether she is considering each option realistically, rather than idealistically
- That she makes her decision without pressure from anyone else, including you, other family members, and the baby's father

When the Baby Is His

If your teen is a boy and he has a sexual partner who is pregnant, our advice is very similar to what you'd do for a teenage girl. In that case, you would:

- **Collect yourself.** Acknowledge that you're shocked (surprised, stunned, whatever) and ask for a moment to collect yourself. Get those emotions in check; you can explore them after his immediate needs are met.
- **Separate your own experience from his.** If you have strong feelings about teen sex, teen pregnancy, abortion, adoption, or teen parenting, you may need to separate your own values from your teen's. Remember, you can't dictate values. He'll need to make his own decision and live with it, so it's important that you give him room to do so.
- **Get a read on your teen's emotions.** Take a moment to assess him and determine how much emotional support he needs from you right now. Consider his emotions going forward. Although the pregnancy isn't happening to him, it likely will affect his life, a fact he may or may not be aware of. He may feel guilt, shame, depression, sadness, like a failure, or overwhelmed at the decisions to be made. He might also feel helpless or frustrated if he's being cut off from the decision-making process. On the other hand, a less mature teen may fail to grasp the enormity of the situation. Offer support or mental health care if he needs it.

- **Tell him you love him.** He may be fearful that you will love or respect him less because he got someone pregnant. Even if you think he knows you love him, take a moment to point out that, regardless of the situation, your love is unchanged.
- **Get more information.** Find out how he discovered that his partner is pregnant, what testing has been done, whether the partner has seen a doctor, whether she has told her parents, and whether she has support at home. If she is under eighteen and lacks support at home, it may be up to your son (and possibly you) to provide it. If she hasn't seen a doctor, encourage your son to get her to do so (and explain why: getting prenatal care early is important for the baby's health if she decides to continue the pregnancy, and, if not, terminating a pregnancy is less risky earlier than it is later in the pregnancy).
- **Remind him about precautions.** Although pregnancy may no longer be a risk, if he has sex with his partner, he should wear a condom for STI protection.

In addition, you can outline the options (above) and the major considerations for him. You can also help him understand that while he may have input, ultimately the choice is not his. But do help him to stay as involved as possible, to communicate openly and honestly about the pregnancy with his partner, and to offer her whatever support he can.

Don't Forget Your Own Needs
Somewhere in this process—after your teen's immediate needs have been met—it's important to address your own emotions as well. You may have suppressed anger, shock, disappointment, or a host of other emotions in order to focus on your teen. So take the time to explore your feelings and talk them through with another adult, keeping your teen's need for privacy in mind, of course. If you're feeling unable to cope, do seek out help. Ignoring your own emotional well-being can make it much harder for you to help your teen.

When She Wants to Make a Baby—and Why

You might view the possibility of a positive pregnancy test as a disaster for your teen—an unplanned event that threatens to derail her future. But your teen may have an entirely different point of view. Although many teens don't have pregnancy in their immediate plans, there are some who view the possibility of becoming a teen parent with anything from ambivalence to elation.

Why would a teen knowingly get pregnant (or get someone pregnant)? We know that teen parents face significant challenges—financially, physically, and emotionally—and difficult choices. But some teens do desire to have a child and don't want to wait to do so. Their reasoning varies (and isn't even necessarily something they've explored for themselves), but some of the possibilities are:

- to create life or "do something productive"
- to have someone in the world who loves them unconditionally
- to prolong or cement a relationship with the baby's other parent
- to seem more adult or to gain independence

Teens who express a desire to get pregnant likely haven't thought through the challenges or taken a hard look at the reality. They may also be focusing squarely on their own needs and desires without considering the needs of their future child.

So how does your teen view a potential pregnancy? You'll only know by asking. This is one of the topics often handed on a silver platter to parents by the media. When teen TV star (and Britney Spears's sibling) Jamie Lynn Spears announced she was pregnant at sixteen (and having the baby) parents everywhere had an open invitation to talk to their teens. Look for such opportunities in the media or the community, or make your own. Ask your teen whether she's thought about how she would feel if she got pregnant (and if she protests that she's not having sex, you can encourage her to suspend reality for a moment and play "what if?"). Would she have an abortion? Give the child up for adoption? Keep the baby?

If she seems ambivalent, unconcerned, or unrealistic about the prospect of becoming a parent, you can offer her some points to think about:

- How do you think having a baby would affect your school plans?
- Have you thought about what would happen between you and your boyfriend?
- Have you ever considered the financial costs of having a baby?
- Have you thought about how you would support a child?
- Do you think you're mature enough to handle the responsibility for another human being?

As with any discussion with an adolescent, try to keep the discussion nonjudgmental. It's more effective to calmly point out inconsistencies than to snarl that she's being foolish. Ideally, you'll help her identify any problems in her thinking, although it might be useful (and even necessary) to seek out professional help.

STIs: THE OTHER KIND OF POSITIVE

Of course, when we're discussing positive tests, pregnancy isn't the only territory to cover. Given that one in four teenage girls has an STI (and most got them from boys), it's possible that your teen will be confronted with a positive result from an STI screening.

Whether or not you're informed about the result is largely up to your teen. In most cases, teens have a right to confidential testing and treatment for STIs, which means you won't automatically be notified if your teen has one. And because there is such a stigma associated with STIs, it's entirely possible that your teen will go through treatment or adapt to living with the disease without ever telling you.

If your teen does tell you, our advice is much the same as it is for parents learning that their teen is pregnant or has fathered a child. You should:

- **Rein in your own emotions.** Focus on your teen's physical and emotional needs first.
- **Separate your values from your teen's.** Rather than preach about safe (or no) sex, focus on getting health care needs met.
- **Assess your teen's emotions and offer support.** How much of an emotional impact there is may depend on the nature of the STI (they may be less upset about an STI that's easily cured than about a more serious health threat or lasting disease).
- **Say "I love you."** This is especially important in cases of STIs that can't be cured, such as HIV or herpes, because a teen may have to live long term with its presence and the fear of your disproval.
- **Get more information.** What did your teen get tested for, and when? Did your teen see a doctor? Were any other STIs screened for? Has treatment started and, if so, what does it involve?

- **Get health care.** If your teen hasn't seen a doctor and hasn't been screened for multiple STIs, make an appointment. A doctor can confirm the test result, screen for other STIs, start treatment, and talk about future STI prevention.
- **Consider the partner(s).** Your teen's partner or partners may already know about the STI, and then again, they may not. Telling someone you have an STI is extremely difficult, but it's an essential next step. Not only can an infected partner continue to infect others, but there also may be serious health concerns that go along with untreated infections. Talk to your teen about why it's essential to tell a partner, and how your teen can do so. Some local health departments or STI clinics can offer advice and help on informing partners.
- **Offer a reminder about precautions.** Wait until the dust has settled a bit and then look at this as a learning experience. But don't use it as an excuse to nag your teen (as in, "Remember the time you got chlamydia because you didn't use a condom?"). Instead, stick with the simple message: To reduce your risk, limit your number of sexual partners, avoid high-risk activities, and use a condom every time you have sexual contact.
- **Tend to yourself.** Up until now, you've been focusing on your teen. Once his needs have been met, however, it's time to think about you. Depending on the nature of the STI, your own history, and the particular situation, you may want to seek help in dealing with your own feelings. This might be in the form of a trusted friend or family member, or it might involve seeing a therapist or counselor to make sure you're dealing with the situation in a healthy way.

CHAPTER 5

Talking to Your Teen:
Finding the Words That Help Teens
Stay Safe

"Don't do it, but if you do ..." If you believe teens should wait to have sex (until marriage, a serious relationship, or just until they're older), saying "but if you do have sex, I want you to use condoms" might seem contradictory. Doesn't it send a mixed message?

Actually, studies have found that it does not. Teens who are encouraged to wait but are also taught about birth control and condoms are no more likely to begin sexual activity earlier than other teens. They are, however, more likely to use contraceptives and condoms the first time they have sex.

And teens themselves say they're not getting a mixed message. In a survey by the National Campaign to Prevent Teen Pregnancy, 66 percent of teens said that encouraging them to delay sexual activity but also providing them information about what to do if they don't delay does not send them a confusing message.[60]

In fact, eight in ten teens in the same survey said they wish they were getting more information about abstinence *and* contraception, rather than one or the other.

Karen's Story

Rachel felt she had a strong relationship with her daughter, Karen. Throughout Karen's teens, the two spent time alone together and had heart-to-heart talks about love and relationships. When the discussion turned to sex, Rachel admitted to her daughter that she'd had sex at the age of sixteen and deeply regretted it. She told Karen that because of her own experience, she really felt it was important for Karen to wait. On the few occasions that pregnancy or STIs came up, Rachel steered the conversation back to her main point: Karen was too young to have sex.

When Karen became sexually active at age seventeen, she and her boyfriend used condoms, but not consistently, and not for sexual activity other than intercourse. Fearing her mother would find out she was no longer a virgin, Karen decided against taking birth control pills or another form of contraception. It wasn't until she had a pregnancy scare that she decided to visit a women's clinic, where she was given a strong message about pregnancy and STI prevention. At the clinic, she got advice on selecting a form of birth control that best fit her needs. From then on, Karen was responsible about birth control and condom use, but continued to rely on the clinic, rather than her mother, for information and support.

Years later, Karen admitted to her mother that she'd never felt she could talk to her about sex. "You told me to wait," she told her mother, "but you never said what to do if you can't wait."

A TIME TO TALK

Teens report that talking to their parents about any part of sex, physical or emotional, is uncomfortable. Still, there's a lot at stake here, so it's worth working past that squeamishness, at least to cover the basics.

If you've checked out your teen's school curriculum and you're satisfied that it's providing reliable information about condom use and pregnancy prevention, there's no need to force a discussion on the nitty gritty, such as symptoms of STIs or how to use a condom. It's okay to back off if you get signs your teen doesn't want—or need—to go there. But do be sure to get across a few key points.

For STIs, be sure to discuss the following:

- STIs are a real risk for any sexually active teen and should be taken seriously.
- STIs aren't just transmitted through vaginal sex; apart from solo masturbation, any sexual contact carries some risk.
- Your body is yours alone, and you should respect it by taking steps to protect yourself from STIs.
- Even if you don't think you have an STI, you have a responsibility to your partner to protect him (or her) by not having unprotected sex.
- Condoms provide some protection from some STIs; therefore, you should use a condom every time you have sex (or insist that your partner does).
- Birth control methods, other than the condom, do not protect against STIs.
- Your level of risk for STIs depends not only on your own sexual activities and history, but also on the sexual activities and history of your partner and their other partners.
- Many STIs have no visible symptoms, so you can't assume someone is "clean" just because they appear to be or say they are.
- As a general rule, if you notice any changes in the skin around or on your genital area—bumps, sores, redness,

itchiness, or discharge, for example—you should have it checked out by a doctor. And don't have sex with someone who has symptoms.

- STIs can have long-term health consequences if they go untreated. Therefore, it's important to seek treatment if you suspect you have an STI. It's also important to tell a partner if you have an STI.

For reduced risk of pregnancy, discuss the following:
- Birth control methods, other than the condom, do not prevent the transmission of STIs.
- To work as intended, birth control methods must be used consistently as directed.
- Dealing with a pregnancy as a teen is almost always extremely difficult, regardless of what you ultimately decide to do. Pregnant teens face tough choices and challenges other teens never have to think about.

If you do opt out of a deeper discussion, give your teen a book you've selected (and read) that explains pregnancy prevention and STI protection in an age-appropriate way (better still if it covers all aspects of sexual relationships). Be sure to ask if your teen has questions, and signal that if so, you're ready to talk.

Pay attention to the verbal and nonverbal cues, too. If your teen grabs the book and dashes off to a bedroom, it might just be a sign of eagerness to get reading. Or she may be too embarrassed to look you in the eye. If your teen is stammering and lingering, it may be that he has questions to ask but feels embarrassed or unsure. Be patient and offer to help him learn more, either by answering questions yourself or by steering him to a reliable website, a doctor, or a trusted family member.

Even if you'd rather your teen didn't have sex, you might also want to provide condoms and permission to use them. It's okay to reiterate your values here. You're not giving carte blanche for indiscriminate sex. You are, however, helping your teen be prepared and responsible in the event that she does have sex.

Birth Control Alert: Beware Those Relationship Transitions

Although teens are perfectly capable of long-term relationships, in general teen relationships tend to be shorter than those that occur in adulthood, which means sexually active teens may have in-between times where they're not actually having sex.

For anyone who sees birth control as a bother, the end of a relationship may seem like a good time to ditch the pill or pass on the patch. That's not a problem with most nonhormonal methods such as condoms, the sponge, or a diaphragm, which start working the minute you apply them. But hormonal methods aren't effective immediately—it can take several weeks before they offer protection against pregnancy—which may mean your teen will be unprotected in the early days of a new sexual relationship.

If your teenage daughter opts for a hormonal method, be sure to talk to her about continuing its use between relationships or about the need to use additional protection if she stops and starts again. When you talk to your son about birth control, make sure he has the facts on how birth control works.

Teen Targeted: Birth Control and STI prevention

Under 15: To teens this age, everything that goes into safer sex—being seen by a doctor, using birth control, taking steps to avoid STIs—may seem overwhelming or even "gross." The burden of those responsibilities are a good reason to delay having sex, but do emphasize that teens who don't delay having sex need to act responsibly. Keep in mind that teens this age aren't able to think ahead as well as older teens are, so although you should talk to them about how pregnancy and disease might affect their future, you shouldn't expect them to fully grasp the ramifications.

15 to 17: At the lower end of this age group teens may still be unable to fully comprehend how their actions will affect their lives. But as teens near adulthood, they become more focused on the future—and more able to plan for it, although they still may have impulsive behavior and experience poor decision making at times. Give them all the information they need to stay safe, but encourage them to think about the future. What are your teen's life plans? Is college in the future? A particular career? A family? Then get your teen to ponder how an unintended pregnancy or even an STI might affect those plans. Even for boys, there are consequences, some of which are long term (supporting a child or living with an incurable disease, for example).

18 and over: Teens this age possess better impulse control and decision-making skills, but there's still the risk of unintended pregnancies and STIs. Remember, two-thirds of the teens who get pregnant every year are eighteen to nineteen years old. And with each additional sexual partner, teens increase their risk of contracting STIs. So remind them about using birth control and condoms, reducing their number of partners, and avoiding high-risk sexual activities.

One Way to Say It ...

Dad:

I think you know that Mom and I believe that sex should wait until you're in a serious relationship. But I really want you to know that if you do have sex, what's most important to us is that you're safe.

Tom:

I know, Dad.

Dad:

Good. So just in case, I bought you these [handing him a box of condoms]. Just for practice or for when you really need them. That's all. You don't have to talk about it if you don't want to, but if you have any questions, I'm here.

Another Way to Say It ...

Mom:

Nina, I found a used condom in the toilet. I'm concerned that it's yours. Can we talk about this?

Nina:

It wasn't mine.

Mom:

I don't see a reasonable explanation for how it could have gotten there if it's not yours, but I don't want to get into an argument about it. You're only sixteen. It seems really young to me. But if you're having sex, I want to be sure you're thinking it through and doing what's best for you.

Nina:

Well, actually, I wanted to talk to you about it, but I didn't want you to be mad. Jeff and I did have sex, but we really love each other.

Mom:

I know you two care a lot about each other. And I guess although I'm sad to hear you're having sex, because it's not what I would have chosen for you, I'm glad that you did use a condom. I worry about pregnancy and diseases.

Nina:

Well, me too, but we're being careful.

Mom:

Have you thought about what you might do if you got pregnant?

Nina:

I wouldn't have an abortion. We would just get married probably and have the baby.

Mom:

Have you two talked about this?

Nina:

A little bit.

Mom:

That's really important, Nina. I'm not in a position to raise a child for you, so you'd be the one doing it. And have you talked about sexually transmitted diseases or how many partners he's had?

Nina:

It was the first time for both of us, Mom.

Mom:

Okay. But I think it's a good idea to make an appointment with your pediatrician so you can talk to her about medical issues, including birth control and getting tested for any diseases in the future. Would you like me to do that?

Nina:

Okay, that's fine, I guess. I think maybe I should go on the pill anyhow.

Mom:

Well, honestly, this is kind of emotional for me. I need a little time to digest that. But your doctor can talk to you about it. Let's make an appointment and then sit down and talk more tonight, when I've had a chance to think. I want to go over the rules of the house, and maybe we can talk about how you feel about what's happened and where things are going with Jeff ...

Ask the Expert: Rumors about STIs

Q: There's a rumor going around my sixteen-year-old's school that a bunch of kids have herpes. I heard it from another parent, and nobody is naming names, but there's a lot of whispering and terrible things being said about the boys and girls in his class. I don't know if it's true, or if they're saying anything about my son (or even if he's had sex), but I'm really upset about the whole thing. I'm not sure what I should do.

A: First, put the situation into context: this is a rumor (unsubstantiated) coming from a place where rumors are more common than complaints about Friday's pop quiz. What you're hearing is second- (or third-, or fourth-) hand, and may or may not be true. Second, recognize this as a golden opportunity to talk to your teen about STIs and safer sex. If you've heard the rumor, you can almost guarantee that he has, too. Even though it may be nothing more than talk, you can use it to open a conversation.

When you do talk, follow these guidelines:

Don't make assumptions. Parents tend to assume that their teen couldn't have an STI (because he's too smart, too careful, doesn't associate with "that sort" of person, etc.). But STIs can affect anyone who has sexual contact (in some cases, even if a condom was used). So, unless you know for a fact that your teen has not had sexual contact, you can't assume he is STI-free. This is true even if he's been tested for STIs, since tests only offer a snapshot in time. Don't assume the rumor is true, but also don't assume that teens at school don't have STIs. Doing so sends the message that the idea of him having an STI is so foreign or offensive to you that you can't even consider it. And that may keep him from coming to you in the event that he ever does have an STI.

Restate your values. As we've mentioned several times in the book, it's good to tell your teen about your values, provided that you don't preach and do allow him to determine for himself what his values will be. If you think he should wait to have sex, say so. But also tell him that if he does have sex, his health and safety are your biggest concern.

Ask him what he's heard. He might echo the rumor as you heard it, but he might also have another story entirely. In addition, he might have questions, so this would be a good time to ask if he does.

Talk about safer sex and STIs. Use the guidelines in this chapter to talk about condom use, types of infections, what to do if he has symptoms, and more.

Put him in touch with resources. If he hasn't already seen his pediatrician or adolescent medicine specialist to talk about safer sex and birth control, now is the time. Offer to make an appointment so he can get a checkup and have his questions answered.

Don't play guessing games. And don't point fingers. It's highly unlikely that you'll be able to determine how true the rumor is, and it probably doesn't matter anyhow. When talking to your teen, focus on STIs and safer sex in general, rather than the details of the rumor.

Try some damage control. If you're upset, other parents probably are, too. And their teens may be confused or full of questions. Since rumors frequently spread incorrect information, it might help to organize an educational effort. Talk to your son's school to see whether they're aware of the rumor, and whether they have taken any action. They may have plans to incorporate a new discussion of STIs into existing sex-ed classes. Or they may see the need to investigate or alert health authorities. In addition, you may want to talk to the school, the parents' association, or another local community group about hosting safer sex, or "talking to your teen," sessions for parents.

A MESSAGE NOT TO MISS

Whether you're engaging your teen in a full discussion of birth control and STIs or just going with the Cliff Notes version, you should make an effort to talk about the rights and responsibilities of being sexually active.

When talking to your teenage daughter, note that if she's going to have sex, she should:

- protect herself from pregnancy and STIs every time she has sex.
- verbally give her consent to her partner so there is never any confusion about what she wants to do and doesn't want to do.
- remember that abstinence is always a valid choice. She always has a right to say no and can decide to stop being sexually active at any point.
- come to you if she ever feels she has been a victim of sexual assault or is in any way uncomfortable with something that has happened.
- come to you if she ever has a health problem, such as a pregnancy scare, an actual pregnancy, or an STI.

For boys, note that he should:

- protect himself and his partner from pregnancy and STIs every time they have sex.
- get his partner's verbal consent before they have sex. He should understand that no means no, but silence doesn't mean yes. Only yes means yes, and for the sake of both parties, it's best for the yes to be verbal.
- remember that abstinence is always a valid choice. He always has a right to say no and can decide to stop being sexually active at any time.
- understand that his partner has a right to say no at any time. That means a partner can say no after having said yes before, or after getting undressed, or after engaging in activities that seem to be leading to sex. In fact, eight states now have laws

that allow a person to withdraw consent even *after* sex has started.

- come to you if he ever feels he has been a victim of sexual assault or is in any way uncomfortable with something that has happened.
- come to you if he ever has a problem, such as a partner's pregnancy scare, an actual pregnancy, or an STI.

One Way to Say It . . .

Mom:

You know that my values are that sex should wait until you're married. And that's really important to me. But what's most important to me is that you stay safe. Do you want to talk about what that means?

Laurie:

Mom, I already know that stuff. I learn it at school, and also there's tons of stuff on the Internet.

Mom:

Okay, that's fine. We don't have to talk about that stuff right now, but if you want to later, I'm here. For now, though, I do want to go over something really important. It's sort of a mini–Bill of Rights for you to remember when you do decide to become sexually active.

Laurie:

This sounds really dorky.

Mom:

The title, maybe, but the rest is really important. Seriously.

Laurie:

Okay, what is it?

Mom:

First, you have a right and responsibility to protect yourself from sexually transmitted infections and pregnancy every time you have sex. Second, you always have a right to stop, no matter how far things have gone or whether or not you've had sex with that person before. In fact, you have a right to decide to stop having sex altogether if that's what is best for you. Third, you have a right and a responsibility to say out loud what you want to do. Nodding doesn't count and neither does saying nothing. Your partner should ask and you should say yes or no. It's a matter of respect, and also it helps make sure there's never any confusion about what you really want to happen. And finally, you have a right to come to me if you ever have any problem, if you feel someone has done something wrong to you or you're worried about being pregnant or having an STI, anything. I may be upset, but what I care about most of all is that you're safe and happy and healthy.

Laurie:

Okay, I guess it makes sense. I mean, I'm not even having sex now, but if I do I'll try to remember that.

Mom:

Well, I think we should keep talking about it. Having sex is a big decision and being sexually active comes with a lot of responsibility. It's not something that you can deal with in one conversation anyway.

Laurie:

Yeah, okay, I get it Mom.

SAFE SUBSTITUTES

Although some parents have a tough time with the concept of their teen masturbating, or engaging in any sexual behavior, it's not realistic to expect that a human will have no sexual outlet whatsoever. And since solo sexual activity and certain partnered activities have no risk of pregnancy or STIs, they can be a reasonable compromise for someone who isn't ready for inter- course—or who just wants to say no on any given day.

Your teen won't likely want to talk about masturbation unless he has questions about whether it's normal to masturbate or concerns about its health effects. But you should know that masturbation is common and has no harmful effect.

Partners can also be sexually active without sharing bodily fluids or having close genital contact. The popular term among many sexual health advocates is outercourse. It refers to a host of activities, from mutual masturbation to phone sex, fantasy sharing, erotic role-playing, sensual massage, and dry sex (imitat- ing sex without removing your clothes).

The vast majority of parents would not feel comfortable suggesting such activities to their teens as a substitute for sex ("I think you're too young to have sex. Why don't you try phone sex instead?"). And most teens would be mortified if a parent dared.

But your teen might have questions about alternatives to intercourse; listen closely for hints that she wants to hear more, and be ready to remind your teen that:

- **Sexual play takes discipline.** In the heat of the moment, it may be tempting to progress to intercourse, even though that's not what you planned on.
- **Safety precautions may still be necessary.** If you're touching genitals or fluids, there's still a risk of contracting an STI. Ideally, anyone touching anyone else's genitals or bodily fluids should wear gloves, although realistically that's a tough sell for most people.
- **It's not emotionally risk-free.** Outercourse is by nature fairly intimate, and therefore may carry some of the same

emotional risks as intercourse. Before engaging in any sexual play or activity, teens should consider the emotional consequences as well as the physical.

PUTTING THE BRAKES ON

When you remind your teen that it's okay to say no at any time, it makes sense to offer a few ways to say it. Toss around some phrases your teen can use to help keep a sexual situation from escalating.

Phrases that work:[61]

- "I think you're cute (or hot, or fine, or whatever term suits her), but I only want to kiss."
- "I've decided that sex isn't right for me right now."
- "I want to wait until we know each other better."
- "I know we've fooled around, but that's all I want to do. I'm not ready to have sex."
- "This is moving a bit fast. Let's stop here for now."
- "This is getting kind of heavy. I need a little time to cool off."
- "No."
- "I want you to stop."
- "I need to go home right now."

For those times they feel pressured to do something that's out of their comfort zone:

- Be very clear about what you want. Saying, "I don't want to have sex," firmly and clearly, leaves little room for doubt.
- Don't feel guilty for saying no. You are responsible for your body. That trumps any responsibility you have for not hurting other people's feelings or disappointing them.
- Don't feel like you have to debate the merits of your decision. Your reasons are your own, and you do not have to justify them to someone else.
- If someone isn't accepting or respecting your decision, repeat it and let them know the conversation is closed.

- If you're still under pressure, find a way to remove yourself from the situation.

Although the perception is often that boys want to have sex all the time, they can feel just as conflicted as girls. They may feel under pressure from friends, a sexual partner, or society in general to become sexually active before they're ready. The above conversation, then, is just as applicable to them as it is to girls.

But it's also true that boys are more likely than girls to be accused of taking advantage of a sexual partner or proceeding without consent. Boys can use the following phrases to verify with their partner that a particular activity is consensual and pleasurable:[62]

- "I'd really like to kiss you. Would that be okay?"
- "Is this all right with you?"
- "Hey, are you comfortable with this? Just checking."
- "Do you want to keep going or stop here?"
- "Would it be okay if we went farther?"
- "It seems like you want to have sex, but I want to be sure it's okay. Is that what you want?"

Of course, your teen might be thinking, "If I stop to ask, she's going to say no." And he may be right. It's entirely possible that stopping to get approval will result in a partner deciding not to let the activity continue. It's okay to acknowledge this and ask your teen to think about what it means. Does he really want his partner to have sex with him only because she feels pressured to do so? How would he feel if that happened to his sister or someone else he loved? Is it worth the risk of hurting someone?

TALKING TO A PARTNER

Asking soon-to-be bedmates whether they have any STIs, have been tested for STIs, or have had risky sex isn't exactly romantic, no matter what your age. It can be doubly awkward if you're a teen, dealing with topics you've never before been exposed to and feelings you've never had. It's no surprise, then, that only about 50 percent of teens say they talk to a partner about contraception and STI protection before they have sex for the first time.[63]

Most people would agree that as cringe-inducing as it is, the pre-sex talk is almost always less awkward than getting a call from your partner weeks or months after the fact he or she has an STI or is pregnant.

Even if your teen has already had sex without the pre-sex talk, now is the time for a reminder that talking to a sexual partner before sex is a must. After all, teens are responsible for their own health and well-being. Try to avoid preaching. It might be tempting to say, "If you can't talk with Tom about something as personal and difficult as pregnancy prevention and sexual history, then you really aren't ready to have sex," which is, granted, true. But such a statement is a conversation stopper. Your teen is having sex, ready or not.

If you handle this part of the discussion well, your teen might even embrace the pre-sex talk as a required milestone on the path to sexual maturity. You can point out that a pre-sex talk has a lot of benefits:

- Like most good communication, it can strengthen the bond between partners.
- It can reduce the stress caused by worrying about diseases and pregnancy.
- It can help you gauge your partner's maturity and sense of responsibility and can convey to your partner that you care about her health and your own.
- It can pave the way for candid discussion should future concerns arise.
- It increases the likelihood that you'll use protection. Research shows that couples who talk about STI and pregnancy prevention are more likely to use contraceptives and condoms.[64]

After you've gone over the benefits, discuss how your teen can have a pre-sex talk. First, you might want to clarify that the pre-sex talk should actually be called the pre-pre-sex talk, because it should happen long before the sex itself. The heat of the moment, when both parties are aroused and ready for sex, isn't the ideal time to hit a partner with a query about whether he has any unexplained rashes or penile discharge. (Of course, sometimes, right before the act is the only time to talk, in which case, they should cool off and have a frank discussion about what's about to happen.)

But what exactly should your teen ask—and say? For starters, couples should talk about:

- Their values: How each views premarital sex, birth control, condoms, pregnancy, and abortion.
- STIs: Whether each has been tested for STIs, which STIs, and what the results were. Does either have any unusual symptoms or concerns at the moment or in the recent past? Is there any reason to believe either might have an STI, even without symptoms?
- Sexual history: How many sexual partners has each partner had and were condoms used consistently?
- High risk behavior: Has either participated in any high-risk behaviors, such as intravenous drug use or unprotected sex with other partners?
- Pregnancy and STI prevention: What method of birth control and STI protection will they use when they have sex?

If a partner's answers cause concern, or seem incomplete or untruthful, it's time to back up and slow down. That gives both parties a chance to find out more and proceed with caution.

NO COVER, NO ENTRY: NEGOTIATING CONDOM USE

Teens are masters at coaxing their parents into a later curfew or sweet-talking them into dropping cash on those pricey jeans that everybody's sporting, but when it comes to insisting a partner wear a condom, they may crumble at the first sign of resistance.

Not that we're badmouthing boys. Many do wear condoms and do so willingly. After all, they're getting the same messages about disease and pregnancy prevention as girls are. There are, without question, teenage boys who would forgo sex because there's no condom available—only to find themselves at odds with their partner. And there are plenty of teens, male and female, who have no problem standing their ground.

But with no guarantees of how a teen will handle the heat of the moment, it's a good idea to equip yours with effective phrases when negotiating condom use.

Below are some of the common protests to using condoms and respectful responses, according to the American Social Health Association (www.ashastd.org).

"I don't have any kind of disease! Don't you trust me?"
"Of course I trust you, but anyone can have an STI and not even know it. This is just a way to take care of both of us."

"I don't like sex as much with a rubber. It doesn't feel the same."
"This is the only way I feel comfortable having sex—but believe me, it'll still be good even with protection! And it lets us both just focus on each other instead of worrying about all that other stuff ..."

"I'm (or you're) on the pill."
"But that doesn't protect us from STIs, so I still want to be safe, for both of us."

"I didn't bring any condoms."
"I have some, right here."

"I don't know how to use them."
"I can show you—want me to put it on for you?"

"Let's just do it without a condom this time."
"It only takes one time to get pregnant or to get an STI. I just can't have sex unless I know I'm as safe as I can be."

"No one else makes me use a condom!"

"This is for both of us ... and I won't have sex without protection. Let me show you how good it can be—even with a condom."

GLBTQ: SAFER SEX

Sexual activity is pretty much the same regardless of your orientation or gender identity, and therefore gay, lesbian, bisexual, transgender, and questioning (GLBTQ) teens will have many of the same concerns, risks, and behaviors as their straight counterparts. But because certain sexual behaviors are riskier than others (anal sex, for example) and because GLBTQ teens may have specific medical or social questions that their straight counterparts won't have, it's a good idea to put them in touch with resources geared toward the GLBTQ community.

If there is a gay community locally—check PFLAG (Parents, Family & Friends of Lesbians and Gays) online (www.pflag.org) for local chapters and resources—it's a good idea to connect with it. Such groups can offer parents emotional support and can be a boon for teens, who can find information and support they may not get elsewhere. A local support network can also help parents and teens on their next step—finding a gay-friendly doctor who can talk about safer sex, screen for STIs, and provide other reproductive health care.

If you don't have a recommendation for a doctor, talk to your teen's pediatrician or family medicine doctor about how comfortable she is in working with gay teens. Not all doctors are well versed on GLBTQ teens' needs. You may find that another doctor in the practice—or another practice entirely—has more experience or comfort in working with gay teens.

Even teens who are connected with the best resources should still hear from their parents about safer sex. A few dos and don'ts for such conversations:

- Don't assume teens are sexually active just because they identify as gay (or lesbian, bisexual, transgender, or questioning). Orientation refers to attraction rather than activity.
- Do talk about birth control, even if your teenage daughter identifies as lesbian or your son identifies as gay. Research has shown that, for a variety of reasons, GLBTQ teens have higher rates of teen pregnancy than their straight counterparts. That may be due to abuse or pressure to have sex with males to prove to themselves or others that they're "normal." Everyone should know how to prevent a pregnancy, even if they never need to put that knowledge into action.
- Do talk about more than just HIV prevention. Although it's often the first disease that parents fear for their GLBTQ teens, it's by no means the only one and isn't even the most likely one. A GLBTQ teen needs to take the same precautions as a straight teen in preventing the entire range of STIs.
- Do talk to your teen about physical safety. GLBTQ teens may face harassment or even violence, and therefore it's important to talk to teens about taking safety into consideration before divulging their orientation. Present this as a matter of practicality rather than something that should instill fear and shame.

CHAPTER 6

What's Love Got to Do with It?
Helping Your Teen Navigate
the Emotional Terrain

What's love got to do with it? Everything, actually. When it comes to emotions, love is a powerhouse. And love expressed sexually in the context of a healthy relationship is one of life's great gifts.

But when it's misused—treated too casually, wielded by someone who intends to manipulate, or simply employed by someone too young or immature to handle the consequences—sex has the power to hurt.

After all, sex tends to heighten the intensity of our feelings and raise the emotional stakes. That's true whether you're sixteen or sixty-six, but for teens, the intensity of emotions sparked by sex, and the complex situations created by being sexually active, are all new.

Without the perspective of someone who has been there before, teens are forced to learn lessons the hard way. They may be naive or unskilled at navigating complex relationships. They may have unrealistic expectations or misinterpret a partner's actions. They may miss cues that they wouldn't miss later in life.

As if that weren't challenging enough, teens are tackling all this at a time when they're already emotionally vulnerable, transitioning as they are from childhood to adulthood. In the teen years, they're figuring out who they want to be and developing a value system that will one day guide them in decision making.

You might have a teen who gets emotionally "hurt" or makes decisions that later cause her to feel regret, shame, or guilt. Or you may have a teen who experiences a rapidly changing mix of emotions, with happiness spilling over into guilt or jealousy. The range of emotions—and the ones that stand out—determine whether a teen ultimately views these early experiences as positive or negative.

But doesn't a little heartache fall into everyone's life? Isn't it part of what makes us who we are? Well, yes—and no. Heartache does happen, and it's not always a bad thing. We may actually learn what *not* to do by experiencing the fallout of certain actions. And with heightened emotions, we also have much to gain. If we never took a chance on love, we'd never have a shot at those powerful, life-affecting relationships that help make us, well, us.

But getting hurt at a young age, or repeatedly, or severely, can have lasting effects—lowered self-esteem and fear of forming attachments are two possibilities—especially for someone who is still developing a sense of self-esteem and self-worth. So while parents can't expect teens to make it to adulthood emotionally scratch-free, they *can* guide teens to make sound decisions that will lessen the chances of feeling lasting emotional pain and improve the chances of growing into an adult who has the ability to be in healthy relationships.

Ryan's Story

Ryan was a seventeen-year-old high school senior who was dating Leah. After two months they had exchanged "I love yous," and shortly after that, they started having sex. Leah called and text-messaged Ryan frequently and spent all of her free time with him. Although he'd always been devoted to playing soccer for the high school team, Ryan sometimes missed practice to be with Leah. He also spent less time on his homework and with friends so that he could be with her.

Ryan's parents had talked to him about sex several times over the years, starting with a discussion about what it was, and leading up to several talks about how they viewed sex—as a healthy part of life, but one that should preferably wait until marriage, or at least until a couple is in a serious relationship that's headed toward marriage. They were aware of Ryan's relationship with Leah, and although they hadn't discussed with Ryan whether the two were having sex, they suspected it. Neither disapproved of the relationship, but Ryan's mother tried to nudge him toward other activities from time to time as a reminder that there was more to life than Leah.

Leah and Ryan hadn't talked directly about their future, but Leah hinted that she thought they'd one day get married. Ryan wasn't sure about that. He didn't plan to get married until after college, but he did feel that he loved her and was committed to her.

However, six months into the relationship Ryan was starting to miss his old social life. Although he still felt love for Leah, he was ready to hang out more with his friends and spend a little less time with her. Leah resisted and the two fought frequently over how Ryan should spend his free time. Eventually Leah broke up with him, saying she didn't think he was truly committed to her.

At first, Ryan was a little relieved to have a way out of the constant fights. But when Leah started dating some-one else, Ryan felt angry and jealous. At home he was mopey and disengaged. At school he was distracted and fidgety. How, he wondered, could I be so easily replaced? Didn't she love me the way I loved her? Is she having sex with him, too?

Ryan didn't want to admit his feelings to his friends, so talking to them about it was out, and he was embarrassed to go to his mother. But his mother gently prodded him. "You seem really sad these days," she said one evening over dinner. "Want to talk?"

Ryan was curt at first, telling her he was just tired from school, but eventually he opened up and admitted he was upset about Leah.

His mother couldn't solve the problem, but she did listen. She noted that the two seemed to have strong emotions for each other and that being part of that probably felt good to Ryan. But she also pointed out that Leah hadn't been entirely reasonable in her demands on Ryan's time and attention. Did she really seem like such a good fit for him? Could it be that maybe "being in love" was what he was missing? And could his jealousy be more about being the object of someone's affections rather than about Leah herself? She didn't mention sex, because Ryan hadn't brought it up, but she did note that sometimes people get swept up in the intensity of the relationship and that when it ends, it is painful.

Ryan's mother didn't push him to respond but asked him to think about it. Ryan did, and although he still felt jealous, he started to understand that the relationship had some serious flaws. A few months later, he started dating again. This time, he proceeded more slowly, both emotionally and physically.

DEEP BREATH, THEN DIVE IN

After the nitty-gritty discussion of STIs and birth control, you might view talking about emotions as a walk in the parenting park. After all, there's warm and fuzzy territory here—love, affection, companionship. Easy, right?

For some, it may be. Others will long for a little hard science to fall back on. Emotions are complex, after all. What seems monumental to your teen may not seem so to you (and vice versa). And emotions are fluid, especially for teens; what seems like a good idea today may not tomorrow.

So how do you start talking about emotions? As focused as you may be on the negatives, it's a good idea to first acknowledge the positive emotional aspects of sex. You're not giving the green light to rampant sexual activity by admitting to your teen something that's probably already apparent: Sex can feel very good, beyond just the physical pleasure.

There is, in fact, a biological reason behind that truth, and you might want to share it with your teen. Intense feelings of love and attachment help create a lasting bond between two people, which once was essential for survival. That attachment helped make sure the man would stick around during a woman's pregnancy and her baby's early years, a time when both mother and baby were most vulnerable. For most people it's no longer a matter of survival, but the wave of powerful primitive emotion is still there.

Sex, then, can be an important part of an intense, caring experience, especially when it's in the context of a healthy relationship where two people respect and support each other. For teens, an intimate relationship can also provide a self-esteem boost, especially if they come from a family life where love and respect are in short supply. And for adults and teens alike, it can fulfill a very human need for physical affection and contact.

One Way to Say It ...

Mom:

When I was young, my mom really focused on how terrible sex is for people who aren't married. She made it sound really awful and said it's not good until you're much older.

Paige:

That sounds like Tammy's mom. She told Tammy if she has sex she'll hate it because her boyfriend won't know what to do, and then she'll probably get diseases, too.

Mom:

Wow, I don't think that's how I'd approach it. I mean, really, sex can be an amazing way to express and share your love. And it definitely can feel very good. Not just the sex part but just being close to someone and having the rush of emotions that goes with that. It can be intense. It can feel really good to love and feel loved, too.

Paige:

Yeah.

Mom:

But that's all assuming that you're with the right person and you're both ready for that intensity and all the things that can happen when you have sex. You know, if you're not in a healthy relationship, and you're not ready to handle the emotions or the responsibility of preventing a pregnancy or sexually transmitted disease, you can really get hurt. Maybe that's why Tammy's mom made it sound so bad. Sex isn't something you can take lightly. Having sex with someone is a really serious step.

Healthy Relationships

Of course, all this discussion is in the context of a *healthy* relationship. When you're talking to your teen, this is a good time to discuss exactly what a healthy relationship is. How this might come up will vary. If you have specific concerns—maybe your teenage daughter's boyfriend seems overly jealous, or your son seems to be the one carrying all the relationship's weight—you might address them as you talk about what a healthy relationship is. If you don't have specific concerns, you might just broach the subject as a way to get your teen thinking about it and applying it to his own situation.

So what's in a healthy relationship? Obviously, there is no one-size-fits-all relationship mold. Personal preferences vary, so some traits may be a turnoff to one person and a draw for another. But there are some basic components necessary for }a relationship to be healthy for both parties. Generally, healthy relationships are built on the following:

- **Respect:** An appreciation and understanding of who you are, not who someone else wishes you were.
- **Communication:** The ability to talk about your feelings, whether they're good or bad, even if doing so might make the other person uncomfortable or upset.
- **Consideration:** Caring about how the other person feels and doing things—or not doing things—with their feelings in mind.
- **Trust:** The ability to believe your mate and curtail jealousy. Also, the commitment on your part to maintain the trust of your partner by not being dishonest.
- **Room for two:** Each person should have his or her own identity and pursuits beyond those of coupledom or of his or her mate.
- **Responsibility:** Each person should feel a responsibility to avoid willfully hurting the other party. But ultimately each person is responsible for his or her own happiness and shouldn't rely on the other party to provide it.

- **Giving, without strings:** Each party gives—whether it's emotions or material objects—because they want to, not because they want something in return.
- **Fairness:** There is fairness in the relationship in terms of how much each person contributes.
- **Conflict resolution:** Both parties should be willing to resolve conflict through compromise, forgiveness, and understanding. Not only that, but they should be able to consider things from their partner's perspective, even if they don't hold the same view.

Remember, this is a conversation, not a lecture, so reciting the above list isn't your best bet. If you're talking—and your teen is receptive—see whether you can set up the conversation and then let your teen contribute his own thoughts. And if "healthy" seems too stiff and non-teen, you can substitute "good." Just be sure to define it so it's clear you don't mean "good" as in "fun" or "feels good." You're talking "healthy," as in, contributing to both parties' personal growth, providing fulfillment, and not being harmful to either party.

One Way to Say It ...

Mom:

Lilly, you and Caleb are spending a lot of time together. And I think that's great, as long as you're both treating each other right, and as long as the relationship is healthy. But I'm realizing that we've never really talked about what a healthy relationship is. Do you ever think about what's really important in a relationship?

Lilly:

I guess. I mean, Caleb and I have a lot of fun together. That's important.

Mom:

> Yeah, that *is* important. But I think respect is really important, too. He should love you and accept you for who you are. Actually, there are a bunch of things that really have to be there for a relationship to be truly healthy. Can you think of a few?

If that kind of conversation doesn't seem plausible (you have a young teen or a not-so-into-talking teen), it doesn't mean you're sunk. You may, however, have to do more of the talking. The key is making sure your teen understands that not all relationships are healthy and has a grasp on what to aim for (and conversely, what to avoid).

She's an FWB: Should You Worry?

You'll remember from chapter 3 that relationships dubbed Friends with Benefits (FWBs)—sexual relationships among friends or acquaintances, without romantic attachment— are fairly common among young adults today. They've also trickled down to the teen set, so it's possible your teen may get involved as an FWB—if not now, then in the coming years.

So what if your teen is an FWB? First, don't panic. One recent study that tracked 1,700 young adults over several years found that FWB relationships had no negative effect on body satisfaction, self-esteem, or the likelihood that someone will have depression or suicidal thoughts.[65] Still, some experts worry that being in FWB relationships may make it harder for young adults to develop the skills they may later need to succeed in serious relationships.

We would caution, too, that for younger teens, a mismatch in expectations could lead to emotional harm. That's in addition to the physical risk (if one or both partners are having sex with other partners, for example). The lack of a commitment also may complicate the already complicated issue of an unintended pregnancy.

When talking to your teen about the emotional aspects of relationships, you may want to discuss the risks associated with FWBs, whether or not you think your teen is in such a relationship.

Emotional Risks:
- The FWB arrangement requires that both parties have similar emotional expectations and that both are okay with there being no romantic attachment. If your teen is expecting the relationship to graduate to a romantic partnership, he should know that such an outcome is the exception to the rule.
- As in any relationship, talking about the rules is important. Is it monogamous? What are the limits on sexual activity, both inside and outside the relationship? Are there any emotional/romantic rules?
- Since there's often no expectation of monogamy, safer sex and STI testing also become extremely important.
- Since there is an expectation that there will be no long-term commitment, pregnancy prevention becomes extremely important.

You might also want to offer your teen some questions to consider when thinking about FWBs. It's not essential that your teen answer them, at least not out loud, but they'll offer a way to explore the concept:

- What do I find appealing about being an FWB? What do I get out of it?
- What am I giving up by agreeing to be an FWB?
- How do I feel about the person? (Do I like her as a friend but have no romantic interest? Like him as a friend and as a romantic interest? Dislike her as a friend but feel physically attracted? Don't know how I feel?)
- Can I really be intimate with someone without being romantically attached?
- Am I being honest with my partner and myself about my comfort level with this arrangement?
- What happens if I become romantically attached?
- What happens if my partner becomes romantically attached, and I don't feel the same way?
- What kinds of rules do I need to make me feel physically and emotionally safe?
- Can I talk to my partner about STIs and insist he or she be screened before we have sex?
- Can I talk to my partner about birth control, and can I be consistently responsible for preventing an unintended pregnancy?

Tips for Talking about It

All this talk about emotions has the potential to get, well, emotional. That's not a bad thing. As long as it's done in a healthy way, sharing your feelings creates stronger bonds.

But you don't want to let your bias or preconceived notions derail the conversation entirely. Below are a few tips you can use anytime you're in a discussion with your teen (about sex, drugs, school, have at it!):

Be sure to acknowledge your teen's feelings. They're powerful, even if you think they're being misinterpreted or given too much weight. Instead of saying, "You're not in love," you might say, "I know you're attached," and then follow up with your concerns: "I'm worried you might be rushing into a serious relationship," or "I'm worried that you haven't taken enough time to really get to know him."

Listen carefully to what is said. Not only is it respectful—and trust us, your teen will notice—but it will also help you make sure your follow-up comments are an accurate reflection of what your teen expressed.

Let your teen own the problem. Generally speaking, people are more likely to take action to correct a problem if they are able to identify it for themselves. So, instead of saying, "She's being totally unreasonable in expecting you to give up your friends," ask your teen questions that will help him identify the problem—and potential solutions. You might ask, "Are you okay with that?" or "Is this going to satisfy you?"

Ask for permission before proceeding. This signals that you respect personal space and also gives your teen a way to put on the brakes before they feel intruded upon. You might say, "Is it okay with you if I ask you a few questions?" You can also explain why: "I just want to talk about the emotional part of sexual relationships because I remember how hard this was for me at this age," or "I want to make sure you make decisions that are good for you, emotionally *and* physically."

Acknowledge discomfort. If the conversation is moving smoothly and your teen seems comfortable, there's no need to plant the seed of discomfort. But if you're sensing hesitance or if you're feeling a little nervous yourself, do acknowledge it. You might say, "This is awkward for me, but ..." or "I know this is personal, but ..." There's even room for humor. If you and your teen share a similar sense of the absurd, it's okay to loosen up and crack a joke, say, comparing the fun factor of this conversation to a root canal. You might just break the mood. But don't overdo it. If it's forced, it'll be about as funny as, you know, a root canal.

Be firm, but don't force a talk. If your teen doesn't want to talk, ask, "When would be a good time to talk about this, because it's important and I am worried about you (or, I want to understand you)?" If your teen still refuses, respect his wishes, but come back to it later and try again. If you're still met with a big "no," simply share your own thoughts, feelings, and beliefs without requiring your teen to do the same. You can't force a teen to contribute, but you can express your own thoughts with the hope that they're heard and absorbed.

Don't assume you know how your teen is feeling. It's okay to comment that you notice your teen is looking sad, but keep your observations to the obvious. After all, you don't know how another person really feels. Ask open-ended questions and allow your teen to put it into his or her own words.

Keep your tone neutral. If your voice sounds shrill or angry, your teen will pick up on—and respond to—the underlying emotion.

TV to the Rescue!

If you're not sure what to make of *Gossip Girl*, and you can't keep track of who's dating whom on *One Tree Hill*, but your teen has TiVoed every episode and watches religiously, you might want to follow that lead.

We're not saying you should pretend to be a fan—teens have fake detectors and will sniff out faux interest from a mile away—but pop culture can be a goldmine for conversation starters. Maybe it's a character in a lopsided relationship, or one who's dealing with a boyfriend who cheats or is jealous. You don't need much. A good, or not so good, TV drama story line can help illustrate a point or give you a jumping-off spot for a conversation about the emotional side of relationships.

Try bringing up a TV relationship and asking what your teen thinks about it. How healthy a relationship does it seem to your teen? How about the girlfriend's decision to dye her hair blonde because her boyfriend said he always liked blondes? You get the idea.

One Way to Say It ...

Mom:
> Jill, I was flipping through the channels last night and landed on *Real World*. Have you been watching?

Jill:
> Mom, you know I always watch.

Mom:
> I know. I got hooked for a few minutes, too. I'm curious, what do you think about Danny and Claire as a couple?

Jill:
> Oh my God, I couldn't believe he told her she shouldn't go out with her friends. I would dump him in a heartbeat if he said that to me.

Mom:

> Yeah, I thought that was out of line, too. He was so
> jealous. He didn't want to be apart from her for even a
> minute. That's really a mistake. Isolating yourself like
> that in a couple is actually associated with abuse, did
> you know that?

Jill:

> I guess. It's definitely not good.

(It might be good to stop here and not ask too many questions to avoid seeming heavy-handed. Let your teen take the lead—if she doesn't want to continue the conversation now, there will be other opportunities to talk.)

WHEN LOVE HURTS

Now that you've acknowledged the upside to sexual relationships and talked about what's healthy, you can move on to the emotional risks. Again, make it a conversation rather than a monologue. You can start by asking what your teen sees as the emotional risks of being in a serious relationship.

If your teen is stumped, you can offer some suggestions. Use the guidelines below to help steer your teen toward an understanding of the situation. Don't use them as a form of interrogation or intrusion. That will be a conversation stopper, and you'll likely end up with a close-lipped or defensive teen.

Some emotional risks of a sexual relationship (some apply to any relationship):

- **If your expectations about the relationship aren't met, you may feel disappointed.** One example to share: Mike and Lindsay have been hanging out and hooking up, but so far there's been no talk of coupledom. Lindsay is secretly hoping that "taking it to the next level" sexually will make a serious relationship magically take shape. When it doesn't, she is disappointed and hurt. She survives, but the experience makes her wary of getting emotionally involved the next time she meets someone she likes.

- **Your feelings of love or commitment may not be reciprocated.** One example to share: Tom finds himself falling hard for Kim, whom he's been dating for six months. Kim likes Tom but doesn't feel in love. When Reed, a popular and attractive classmate, shows an interest in Kim, she quickly dumps Tom, leaving him heartbroken.
- **There may be negative social fallout from friends, relatives, or acquaintances.** One example to share: Ethan and Olivia hang out in the same social circle and hook up at a party one night. Ethan isn't dating anyone else, but he's been flirting with a host of girls. Suddenly Olivia finds herself on the receiving end of jealous barbs and social snubs from the girls he'd been flirting with, many of whom were her friends.
- **The emotional intensity may lead to poor decision making, such as not using birth control or practicing safer sex.** One example to share: Things between Dylan and Haylee have been heating up physically and emotionally. Dylan feels he's falling in love. Haylee professes the same. They've decided it's too soon in their relationship to have sex, but one night after a romantic date, they find the temptation to be too much. Neither has a condom, but in the heat of the moment they "just get carried away."
- **If your partner isn't trustworthy, he may reveal personal information about your relationship to others.** One example to share: Paige has a crush on Lucas, and after a party one night the two have sex in Lucas's car. Lucas brags about it in a text message to a friend, who shows it to another friend. Before she knows it, Paige finds herself the subject of conversation all over school.

- **If your early experiences in love are strongly negative, you may have a hard time building healthy relationships later.** One example to share: Elizabeth falls in love with Dave, who pressures her to have sex and then cheats on her. Hurt and embarrassed, Elizabeth has had a hard time trusting men since then.

- **You may have to endure the stress of a pregnancy or STI scare, or an actual pregnancy or STI.** One example to share: Brandon gets a call from Lauren. "You gave me chlamydia!" she says. Lauren is angry. Brandon says, "I don't have chlamydia." In fact, Brandon does have chlamydia but doesn't know it. He now must go to a clinic to be tested and treated. Based on his risk factors, Brandon's doctor recommends a full STI screening, which he agrees to. When he's done, he must contact his last sexual partner to tell her to be tested. Then he must wait for his test results. He finds the ordeal stressful, embarrassing, and scary.

Focusing on Your Teen

Now that you've talked in general terms, you can move the conversation toward your teen's own experience. If your teen is in a long-term or steady relationship, you'll likely have an idea of how committed it is. But if not, and you're aware that she is sexually active, it's okay to ask directly whether the sexual activity occurred within the context of a relationship and then to explore the relationship itself more deeply, provided your teen seems open to such a discussion.

The goal is not to "prove" anything, but rather to help your teen explore the issues, either with you as part of the conversation or alone. Another goal is to gather enough information so you have a feel for what's going on in your teen's life and can give guidance if he opens the door, directly or indirectly. Even if you walk away without much more information than you began with—which may be the case if your teen isn't ready to talk— you've set the tone for an open discussion and sent the message that you're involved and available to talk.

Some questions to ask:

- What's your status? Are you two serious? Just hanging out? Somewhere in between?
- Are you seeing each other exclusively or dating other people, too?
- Have you talked about that?
- How is it going?
- Do you two get along?
- Does it seem like you're fair with each other?
- Are you mostly happy in the relationship? Mostly unhappy? Somewhere in between?

One Way to Say It ...

Mom:

David, I noticed that you and Claudia have been hanging out a lot. Do you mind if I ask you some questions?

David:

Mom, it's personal.

Mom:

I know. And I don't mean to pry. It's just that I don't want you to get hurt. I'm just wondering where you two stand. How serious are you?

David:

I don't know. We're just having fun. I mean, we're not dating other people, but I'm not going to marry her, if that's what you're wondering.

Mom:

Well, I guess that's good, since you have a lot of plans for the next few years. Have you two talked about being exclusive, or is it just something you sort of know without having said it?

David:

> We've talked about it. She always tells me I'd better not even look at another girl.

Mom:

> Really? Wow, is she joking or what?

David:

> She's joking, Mom. She's not like that.

Mom:

> Yeah, I've never heard you say she was the jealous type, that's why I was surprised. So, do you feel like things are pretty good with you two?

David:

> It's cool. We just like being together. We keep it light.

Mom:

> Great, I guess as long as you're both okay with that, it's working for you both.

David:

> Yeah, it's working. We have a good time together.

LIKE, LOVE, LUST—OR SOMETHING ELSE?

You might know the feeling: You meet someone new and feel a sudden rush of excitement. You have the same interests, instant comfort with each other, a red-hot physical attraction. Is it lust? Infatuation? Love? Have you found your soul mate, or just your bed mate?

For teens experiencing such feelings for the first time (or third, or fifth), putting a label on it can be particularly confusing. What is love, anyway? And how do you know whether the person you're with is Mr. (or Ms.) Right, or merely Mr. (or Ms.) Right Now?

It's natural for teens to feel pressured to find someone to love forever—a message that's reinforced in the media and pop culture, even for teens and young adults. Sex often gets tied up in the equation; when a teen feels "in love," sex may seem an inevitable expression of that emotion. The question then may become, "How do I know whether I care about someone enough to have sex?" And since teens tend to have shorter-term relationships, it may be a question that comes up again in the near future.

Athough you probably can't come up with a formula for determining whether it is love, you can help your teen consider the issue of whether or not to have sex with any given person. Some questions to think about (and no, your teen doesn't have to answer them out loud):

- Is it a healthy relationship?
- What do I expect emotionally from the relationship once it becomes sexual?
- Is my expectation likely to be met?
- Am I considering sex because I feel pressured to do so?
- Will I feel good about my decision after we've had sex?
- Do I feel ready to have sex with this person?
- Do I trust this person?

As with any decision-making process, it helps to have a clear view of your values. If your teen isn't already clear on her values, there are a few more questions to consider:

- In general, when do I believe it's okay for two people to have sex?
- When do I believe it's clearly not okay?
- What are possible gray areas?
- In general, what do I think is right for me?

Of course, your teen shouldn't forget the safety element: The risk for STIs increases with each sexual partner, and therefore an important part of safer sex is reducing the lifetime number of sexual partners and choosing your sexual partners carefully to avoid those who participate in risky behaviors.

When Your Teen's Head Is in the Clouds

Listening to your teen talk about a first love—or even the fifth—may be hard. The thought of your baby moving into adulthood isn't an easy one to accept. Nor is it easy to shed your protective mom (or dad) persona, which may cause you to view every current or prospective romantic partner as a potential heartbreaker.

And in some cases you may be right. You have the benefit of experience. And since your view isn't clouded by love, you can clearly see your teen's mate's flaws. However, with a few exceptions (we'll get to that in chapter 8), this isn't the time to directly challenge your teen.

Even if you don't like or agree with what you hear, try to suspend judgment and keep your tone neutral. Saying things like, "He's using you," or "You don't really love her" will likely lead to a defensive response and cause your teen to end the conversation, which will leave you with little room for influence. This isn't just because you're dealing with an adolescent. People of any age don't like to hear that they're being deceived, making bad decisions, or being foolish, so tread lightly.

Rather than arguing with your teen over perceptions, point out the contradictions that you see. Instead of saying to your daughter, "He's just using you," point out that his words don't seem to match his actions. If your son declares himself "in love" after knowing someone for a week, acknowledge that attraction can feel like love, but remind him that typically, true love requires a deeper knowledge than you can probably achieve in seven days.

One Way to Say It ...

Mom:

It sounds like you really feel strongly that Jason loves you.

Nina:

He does, Mom.

Mom:

From the outside looking in, it seems like he's not treating you in a loving way, though. I've just noticed that he never sets up dates with you, and then calls you at the last minute when he's free. It seems like he expects you to drop everything but he doesn't do the same for you. Have you noticed that?

Nina:

He does do that, but only because he's really busy with his friends. It's hard for him to get away from them.

Mom:

That's true. He's busy with school, lacrosse, and his job, but you're busy, too. And you would never do that to one of your friends. You just may want to pay attention to how it makes you feel when he does that.

Nina:

Sometimes I get annoyed. But when I'm with him, he's there 100 percent, so it's worth it to me.

Mom:

Okay. I can appreciate that. I just don't want you to get hurt.

Nina:

How can you love anyone without getting hurt?

Ask the Expert: My Incredible, Disappearing Teen

Q: My teenage daughter used to be such an independent spirit. She was the one who insisted on dressing as a pirate for Halloween when all her friends opted for the fairy princess outfit, who wanted to be a beekeeper when she grew up, and who cut her hair short when long locks were all the rage.

Now that she's dating Alex, she seems like a different person. She spends all her babysitting money on clothes that Alex likes and getting her hair highlighted (because Alex likes it that way). She started tae kwon do so she could spend more time with him (Alex does tae kwon do). And half her sentences start with, "Alex says," or "Alex thinks." Argh! It makes me cringe. He doesn't seem like a bad guy, and I don't get the sense that he's forcing her to do any of these things. She seems happy. But I feel like my daughter is being replaced with some sort of robot who only wants to do things to please her man. What do I do? How can I get her back?

A: First, you should applaud your daughter for earning her own money and taking up a hobby that will likely improve her health. Both are positive steps on the path to adulthood.

As for your concern, it's very natural to fear that you're "losing your teen" as she passes through adolescence. In a way, you are. After all, one day soon she'll no longer be a teen. To prepare for that, she has to figure out who she is and how she will present herself to the world. She's also figuring out the mechanics of a relationship, which is a process of trial and error. For now, she's trying on things that please Alex, either because she truly likes those things, or because she likes the positive attention she gets from him.

She may decide eventually that in this case, she bent too far toward someone else's interests and opt never to do so again. But she might also find that she was able to explore herself and her world, and that it served its purpose with no long-term loss of self. Either way, these are things she has to figure out for herself. As long as you don't see signs of an abusive relationship (see chapter 8), you shouldn't try too hard to "get her back."

However, you *can* talk to her about what she thinks, likes, and wants. It will help her better know herself, which is an important step on the path to adulthood.

Consider the following talking points:

Ask her what she likes. In appearances, hobbies, and activities. This may mean gently countering, "Alex loves me in cute little dresses," with, "But what do *you* like?" Opportunities might also arise as you go about your day.

Encourage independence. Think about the messages you send your teen. Do you encourage conformity or individuality? In your family, is it a positive thing to blaze your own trail, or is it a liability? It's a balancing act—bucking the system for its own sake isn't always effective—but you should encourage independent thinking whenever possible. Explain why it's important for your teen to think for herself: because only she can determine what's good for her; because she has a right and responsibility to do so.

Encourage self-reflection. Ask your teen to think about how she feels about herself. What are her strengths and weaknesses? Is she mostly happy with who she is? Or is she feeling inadequate? What would she change and what would she keep? Is she changing who she is so she can please someone else?

Encourage self-reliance. We all like compliments, and it's natural to want to be well regarded by others. But relying on others to validate your decisions or provide a sense of worth can be dangerous. Encourage her to recognize her strengths and feel pride in who she is. Developing your teen's sense of self-worth means she won't have to rely on others to provide it.

ANY REGRETS?

If talking to your teen about the emotional side of a sexual relationship was sparked by an event that caused you concern, you may have some context—whether your teen had random sex, a casual encounter with an acquaintance, or sex as part of a committed relationship. But it's also possible that you're completely in the dark.

If you're concerned because your teen seems hurt or upset over the event, you might try to ferret out some details. Start with a simple, "What happened?" or "What's been going on?" You may not get an answer, or only a bare-bones outline. But you might also be surprised by how much will come out if you create a supportive atmosphere by listening actively. Once the subject is on the table, teens—most of whom admit they're uncomfortable talking to their parents about sex—may actually feel relieved to be able to talk about it with someone they love and respect.

If your teen seems receptive, you can explore how she feels about becoming sexually active or being in a sexual relationship. Remember to be supportive and nonjudgmental. It's natural for a teen, especially a younger teen, to be defiant. Even teens who realize they've made a bad decision may be afraid to admit it to you. Talking it through can help teens gain the comfort and confidence to acknowledge mistakes and learn from them.

Ask your teen:
- Was it something you wanted to do?
- Did you feel pressured or did things get out of control?
- Do you have any regrets about what happened, or how or when it happened?
- Do you think you'd handle it differently if you had it to do over again?
- Have you thought about what you want from this relationship (if there is one)?
- Have you talked to your partner about how you feel?
- How happy are you with the decision overall? Do you wish you'd acted differently?

When teens express regret, you can encourage them to consider what they'd do in the future to avoid a similar situation. Teens will often admit to feeling that "things just got out of control." This can be due to drugs or alcohol, pressure to conform or to please someone, or just a feeling of powerlessness over their own body (teens may say their bodies "took over").

You can also help your teen come up with solutions to potential problems before they happen. Teens are under extraordinary pressure to conform, so you might have to work with yours to find solutions that offer protection without a loss of face. You can even role-play so your teen has certain phrases at the ready.

Some questions to consider together:
Q: What can you do if you're invited to a party, and when you get there, find everyone is drinking?

A: Find some way to leave. "Remember" that you promised to call home at 10 and then report that your mom insists you come home immediately. Or, feign a stomachache/headache/sudden onset of explosive diarrhea (the last one's intended to earn you a laugh) and go home.

Q: What can you say to partner who insists that you do something you don't want to do?

A: Say no firmly and continue to say no for as long as it takes. Make it a relationship breaker if you need to.

Q: What can you do if you find yourself tempted to do things in the heat of the moment but know you'll later regret them?

A: Avoid situations that offer temptation. If making out with your boyfriend on the couch in his basement always leads to a moral tug-of-war, stay out of the basement. Steer your activities toward places where you're around others and can have fun without being tempted to take it further than you're ready to go. If you're tired of hooking up with "Billy" every time you bump into him at a party (because you never hear from him in between parties), find yourself a "Billy"-free zone.

Q: What can you say if others are pressuring you to do something you're not comfortable with?

A: Stand your ground. Say no, and say it like you mean it. Make eye contact, stand up straight, and say it with confidence. Remind them that you're an individual ("everyone's doing it" doesn't apply to you because you're not "everyone"). If they don't respect your limits, it's time to develop a new group of friends. You shouldn't have the stress—especially from friends—of constantly having to defend yourself.

In addition to peer pressure, teens may think that everyone is having sex, for example, when that's really not the case. Give your teen perspective by talking about the realities of teens and sex.

No Regrets—No Kidding

Of course, some teens will tell you they're happy with their decision. They may feel that adding sex to a relationship strengthened their feelings for a partner or made them feel more like an adult. They may decide that a sexual encounter outside of a relationship was not only enjoyable, but empowering. If that's the case, acknowledge those feelings. If the feelings seem genuine and you agree that the partner is a decent human being, share in your teen's happiness.

If your teen is adamant that sex outside of a committed relationship doesn't present emotional problems—and seems to genuinely believe it—make sure your teen is being as safe as possible by limiting her number of sexual partners, using protection and birth control, and choosing partners carefully.

If you are uncertain about whether your teen's statements are genuine, lay the groundwork for more conversations in the future. You might say, "I hope you know that if things ever change, my door is always open. I want you to be happy."

Teen Targeted: Sex and Relationships

Under 15: Younger teens may be more worried than older ones about getting in trouble or upsetting their parents. To get teens to talk, you may have to confront those fears. One approach would be, "I'm upset, but I want to talk about it to make sure you're okay," and even, "I'm not going to punish you for what happened," or, "I'm not sure how we're going to handle the fact that you broke the rules, but I'm more concerned right now with making sure you're okay." When they do talk, they'll probably be most interested in the issues immediately at hand and less focused on the future.

15 to 17: If your teen is inexperienced in relationships, you might steer the conversation toward exploring what the relationship means and how sex has (or hasn't) changed it. Teens this age will be more likely to focus on the future but will still be most concerned with what's going on in the present.

18 and over: Teens this age are old enough to evaluate how they feel about being in a sexual relationship (although if your teen wants to talk about it, by all means, go ahead). This age group may be more open to talking about the future of the relationship, how they'll feel if it ends, and how they plan to handle sex in future relationships.

Does Reputation Matter?

As important as it may be to you that others think highly of your teen, you're not likely to win any points by insisting your teen change his behavior with reputation in mind. Teens aren't likely to see your family's standing in the community in the same light that you do, and they already know that other teens talk and can be cruel.

The exception is younger teens, who may not be capable of thinking through the consequences of their actions. They may, for example, naively assume that what they do will remain private and therefore may be surprised when their partner spills the beans. Or they may not fully anticipate the social fallout from their actions. For those teens, it might be helpful to talk through some of the possibilities.

Even older teens may not fully appreciate the damage that can be done by anyone with a computer or cell phone. Today, incriminating photos and videos can make their way onto the Internet—and out to the entire wired world—almost as fast as you can say "I wish I hadn't done that." Gossip gets a hand, too, through blogs, text messages, and social networking sites.

Growing up in the online age requires reminders that what teens do may not be a private matter for very long.

You don't need to go into great detail, but there are a few points you might want to make with your teen:

- **Gossip happens.** Whether at school, work, or the neighborhood swimming pool, wherever there are groups of people, you can almost guarantee there will be gossip. Sometimes it's based on fact, sometimes not. You can't really stop gossip, but you can be aware that it exists and that your actions, or even the perception of your actions, may be discussed.
- **Things that happen in public aren't private.** With many teens equipped with cell phones that take pictures or even small video clips, the impact of something being made public is greater than ever. Give them the lesson before they learn it the hard way: If you don't want what you're doing to be posted on YouTube tomorrow, don't do it in public. And by public, we mean any place where you are in view of people you don't know well and trust implicitly.
- **Things that are posted online or sent digitally have a way of moving fast.** This applies to words and images. So while it may be tempting to "sext" (send a racy photo via cell phone) your significant other, be aware that it's very easy for the image you send to be distributed. Ditto for images you send via e-mail or post on your "personal" Web page. And once it's out there, you have no way of deleting it or undoing the damage.
- **The double standard stinks, but it's real.** Girls who have sex are sluts, boys who have sex are studs. It's not true, not fair, and not a perception held by everyone, but there are still many people who view sexually active girls as morally loose. That doesn't mean you shouldn't have sex (if you're making informed decisions and acting responsibly). It does mean you should consider how your actions will be perceived and keep your eyes open to all the possible reactions.
- **Homophobia exists.** This will come as no surprise to GLBTQ teens. But even teens who don't identify as GLBTQ may be

questioning or trying on different identities. Talking to all teens about the fact that GLBTQ teens face harassment and even violence because of their orientation or gender identity is helpful in terms of spreading awareness. That said, the potential for a negative reaction doesn't mean GLBTQ teens shouldn't come out or don't have a right to their sexuality. It is simply a reality they should prepare for by knowing their rights (including their school's harassment policy, if there is one) and developing a strong support network.

If you're talking to your teen in response to a particular incident, you shouldn't harp on the reputation issue, as we mentioned above. But you can gently prod a little introspection about the potential reputation fallout from the behavior.

Ask the Expert: Reputation Worries

Q: My sixteen-year-old daughter was suspended from school for violating a school dance policy. She was supposed to be at the dance but snuck out with her boyfriend and was caught engaging in oral sex behind the school. I'm freaked out about her doing what she was doing, obviously, but I'm also angry. Now she has a bad reputation at school. I was so embarrassed when the school called. What kind of parent will they think I am? She not only hurt her reputation, but she hurt mine, too."

A: It's perfectly reasonable for you to feel worried about your daughter and to feel angry about her poor judgment. And it's important when something like this happens to use it as a chance to talk about some things that are very important. First, though, talk to someone to get support for yourself. Then talk to your daughter. Don't let your fears about what others will think or your anger at your daughter put a wall between you and her.

Some ground to cover:

- **Share your values.** If you haven't already expressed to her how you view sex—and we mean all types of sex—do so now. That means being more specific than just, "I'm against anyone your age having sex." Define sex, and then define the behavior you would like to see. You might say, "I think that sexual activity—and that means any kind of intimate contact, including oral sex and touching each other sexually—should wait until you're in a serious relationship and you're old enough to handle consequences such as pregnancy and sexually transmitted infections."
- **Find out what happened and what's happening.** She may not tell you, but if you're nonjudgmental and willing to sit and listen, she just might. You might say, "That's where I'm coming from." And then, "I really care about how *you* feel about what happened." And then ask: "What is your relationship with (name of boy)? What do you want it to be? If you had it to do over again, what would you do differently?" Look at our earlier advice in this chapter on talking about healthy relationships, regrets, and how to avoid situations that lead to trouble.
- **Focus on health.** Maybe her partner wore a condom, but if they dashed out of the dance for a few furtive minutes, chances are he didn't. And even if he did, there's still the possibility of contracting an STI. You also may not know whether she's had or is regularly having intercourse or other sexual contact. Bottom line: It's time to see a doctor, if she hasn't already. Avoid alarmist statements such as "You need to see a doctor to make sure you didn't pick up a disease." And definitely steer clear of abusive language such as "You're a slut." Instead, frame a visit to the doctor as standard procedure (which it is) for anyone who has sexual contact. And be sure to give her the message that her safety and health is your chief concern. She can talk to her doctor about her reproductive health, STIs, birth control, and anything else she'd like to talk about.

- **Establish the expectation that rules will be followed.**
  She broke the rules by leaving the dance: a clear no-no.
  If she's upset and remorseful about the whole thing, you
  might feel tempted to cut her some slack. And certainly
  there's room to do so. But for all rule breaking there should
  be some consequence. (See chapter 7 for more on rule setting and enforcement.)
- **Address the public concern.** You're worried about reputation, and that's natural. But she probably will not respond to
  an attempt to forbid oral sex on the grounds that you think
  she'll get a bad reputation. You might, however, make head-
  way by addressing the secondary concern, which is that she
  was performing a sex act in a public place. You can start this
  part of the conversation by telling her you're worried because
  you know how common gossip is—and how easy it is to
  spread gossip today. Remind her that the double standard is
  alive and well, and while her partner might be getting high
  fives, she's not likely to be seen in the same flattering light.
  Then ask her how she feels now that her friends and classmates know what happened. And what if other guys she liked
  knew about it? What if another student with a cell phone
  camera snapped her in the act and posted it on the Web?

These are all steps you can take with your teen, but they
don't help with your main fear, which is that your daughter will
be taunted, shunned, or branded a "bad girl." Unfortunately,
there isn't much you can do other than offer your daughter as
much support as you can in the weeks and months to come.
She may find the whole thing eclipsed by the next big scandal
(just wait a week, it's bound to happen), but she might also be
dealing with fallout for a long time to come. Check in with her
frequently. Ask how she's doing, if she's happy at school, or if
she wants to talk. You can be supportive without approving
what she did.

And be on the lookout for signs that things aren't going well:
Withdrawing from one social circle can be a good thing if it's

done for self-preservation (and she finds a new social group within a reasonable time), but if she seems to withdraw from all social groups, is frequently sad, experiences a drastic change in grades at school, or frequently misses school due to illness, there may be a more serious issue at hand (see our discussion of depression in chapter 8).

Teen Targeted: Gossip

Under 15: Younger teens are acutely aware of how they're perceived by others, but they're less likely than older teens to think about the consequences of their actions. Get your teen thinking about gossip—how common it is and how quickly and easily it can spread. Offer the rule of thumb that people shouldn't do anything in public that they don't expect to be made public.

15 to 17: Teens this age are still concerned about how they're perceived in their peer group, although they may be less concerned about same-sex peers and more concerned about how they're perceived by future romantic partners (for example, how having multiple partners now might affect later relationships), so you may want to explore that. Keep in mind, though, that boys face far fewer ramifications in terms of reputation than girls do.

18 and over: Teens this age aren't as heavily influenced by their peers. If your teen identifies gossip as an issue, however, you can certainly discuss it.

Sharing Your Own Experience—Or Not

Although most teens probably don't want to hear the intimate details of a parent's first sexual encounter, they might be interested in hearing how you felt about it, especially if you can draw parallels to your teen's situation. You are, after all, a real person, and your experience may hit closer to home than any theoretical example. Plus, if you learned from your experience, there's a good chance your teen can, too.

Teens may even ask how old you were when you first had sex, and who that first partner was. Even if your actions as a teen are counter to your values as an adult, it's not a good idea to lie outright. After all, your teen deserves more respect than that. But there's a fine line between helpful frankness and too much information (TMI, if you're a teen). How much you tell is up to you and your own comfort level. If you're not comfortable at all, you might go with, "That's really personal, and I don't feel comfortable talking about it, but I think it's important for you to know that …" and shift the conversation to your values or lessons you've learned.

If you do tell, it's best to keep it light on details and heavy on meaning. If you had sex at sixteen, there's no need to recount the event—no one really wants to know that much about their mom or dad—but do relate what the experience taught you (if anything). If the relationship soured and you regretted the decision, say so. But be on the watch for freakout signs. If it seems your teen is uncomfortable, switch gears and tone it down. You can shift to relationships the teen has witnessed, whether it's friends or even relatives, or that great fallback, pop culture.

WHEN THE CONVERSATION ISN'T HAPPENING

You want to talk to your teen. You're ready to be nonjudgmental, to listen, and to help. But what if your teen isn't talking back? What if your efforts are met with anger? Or if your teen stonewalls?

If you're getting back-off signals—crossed arms, terse or clipped responses, or outright hostility—it's possible that moving forward could prompt your teen to shut down completely. Instead, table the conversation and try again when your teen has had a chance to calm down. Don't present this as a battle of wills. You're response shouldn't be, "Fine, but we're going to talk about it later" with an implied "whether you like it or not." Stay calm and offer her a reprieve. It might be, "I can see that you're feeling angry right now, so this probably isn't the best time for us to talk." Then follow up with a request to revisit the conversation: "But I really do want us to talk about how you're feeling and what's going on in your life." Offer a reason, such as, "You're making some very adult decisions, and you're still growing and shaping the adult you're going to be one day. I just want us to talk about it so we can both be sure that you're doing what's best for you."

It's okay to acknowledge anger (or disappointment, sadness, or any other emotion) on the side of either party. These are all genuine emotions, and acknowledging them just tells your teen you're human. Just remember to stay calm and respectful, even if you're upset or angry. If you're having trouble containing your own emotions, acknowledge that, too. Explain how you feel and ask to continue the conversation later. Just make sure you follow up and restart the conversation within a reasonable time.

Teen Targeted: Time to Talk

Under 15: Younger teens, who might be at greater emotional risk once a relationship turns sexual, might warrant a firmer parental hand. If your teen doesn't want to talk, offer a limited number of choices for when to revisit the conversation. If the response to "when is a good time for us to talk again?" is "never," you'll need to step in with a set time. "We need to talk, so never isn't an option. Let's try tomorrow at 3 p.m. or right after dinner. Which would you prefer?"

15 to 17: At this age, it's normal for there to be negotiation. It's okay to back off, but put limits on how much room you'll give, and let your teen know that you'll be monitoring the situation. You might say, "I just want you to know that I'm here for you if you're ready," and then follow up with, "but if it starts to affect your grades because you're upset and can't sleep at night, then we need to sit down and talk."

18 and over: If your teen doesn't want to talk, don't force it. Focus on sending the message that you're there to talk if your teen needs you or to connect your teen with someone else who can help.

CHAPTER 7

No, Mark Can't Sleep Over:
Why Rules Are Important to Establish and Enforce

So you've come to terms with the reality that teens have a right to make certain decisions about what they do with their bodies. You've shared your values, talked about safety, answered questions, and stand ready to support your teen. You know that declaring "You're not allowed to have sex" is a doomed approach. Congratulations.

But your job is not done. Giving your teen an increasing degree of independence doesn't mean giving up all authority. In fact, because you're allowing your teen the leeway to make more decisions, it's important that you establish, discuss, and enforce the appropriate boundaries. It might be comforting to know that although they're masters of moaning and groaning, most teens expect, accept, and desire the security of such structure. It decreases anxiety. Research also consistently shows that parents who establish and enforce rules typically have teens who are less likely to get involved in risky behaviors.

WHAT'S YOUR PARENTING STYLE?

Maybe you grew up in a family where the rules were nonnegotiable or, conversely, where there were no rules at all. Maybe you felt the restrictions were unyielding and unfair—or longed for a little more guidance on how to behave. Your background no doubt has shaped how you handle setting and enforcing rules in your own family. You might find that you're most comfortable following a pattern similar to the one you experienced in childhood, or that you're determined to do the opposite.

Other factors—such as your teen's temperament, your family dynamic, and what you've found to be effective in the past—will also impact your parenting style. But it's worth taking a moment to think about parenting styles and what has been shown to work.

One well-established theory of parenting styles was developed in the 1960s by clinical psychologist and researcher Diana Baumrind, who described four distinct styles:

The permissive parent. Permissive parents typically are warm and loving but have low expectations for compliance with rules. In fact, they make few demands of their children, either because they're too busy or they want to avoid conflict. They may strive to create an environment that more closely resembles a friendship than that of parent and child.

The neglectful parent. This is like the permissive style but is characterized by a more pervasive lack of involvement in a child's life. It can be very damaging, as children grow up without the reinforcement of a loving environment and also without the structure provided by rules and boundaries.

The authoritarian parent. In this style, parents lay down the law and refuse to negotiate or communicate openly. They might declare, "Do what I say, because I say so." Authoritarian parents discourage independence. In some cases, for families in dangerous inner-city environments, for example, there is evidence that an authoritarian style can be effective. But in almost every other setting the authoritarian style backfires, and parents and their children become entangled in a power struggle. This style can damage your relationship with your teen in the long run and results in missed opportunities to share your wisdom and experience.

The authoritative parent. In this style, parents communicate openly and negotiate with their children. They encourage independent thinking but also set high expectations for rule following. They are strict but give reasons for their rules. In most cases, this is considered the healthiest and most effective parenting style. Authoritative parenting tends to produce children who are disciplined, have self-control, and do well academically and socially. When it comes to sexual activity, the children of authoritative parents are less likely to engage in risky sexual behavior, less likely to become pregnant, and more likely to use condoms.[66]

Which type of parent are you? Ideally, you'd fall squarely within the authoritative model, but in real life, the lines can sometimes be blurred. You might be authoritarian in some respects, but authoritative in others. Or authoritative, but sometimes permissive. As you think about setting and enforcing rules with your teen, keep the authoritative model in mind and remember to:

- **Communicate openly about the rules and the reasons behind them.** It shows your teen respect, and you'll have a better chance of compliance if your rules seem reasonable.
- **Negotiate.** As your teen gets older and earns the right to more responsibility, negotiating becomes more important.
- **Set high expectations for rule following.** Everyone makes mistakes or has occasional lapses, but you should expect more than 80 percent compliance the first time you lay down the law, and more than 95 percent compliance after the second or third request.
- **Be consistent in enforcing rules.** Big slip-up or small, if it's important enough to be covered by a rule, it's important enough to be enforced.
- **Trust your teen, but provide supervision as well.** Supervision shows you care, provides protection, and also allows you to increase your teen's independence in a controlled way.

Keep a Watchful Eye

Your teen has been growing up (and away) for some time now. Maybe your daughter is wrapped up in her social circle, or is busy with school and extracurricular activities. Or maybe your son is deeply immersed in sports, studying, or practicing with his basement band. You know their friends, eat dinner together, and even squeeze in a little fun time together when your schedules permit. But although your teen occasionally unloads on you—giving you the latest head-spinning who-did-what-to-whom report, for example—you're pretty sure you're not seeing the whole picture.

It's natural to wonder what those missing pieces are. Is your teen doing things that would make you cringe? Is it safe to assume your daughter is at the library because that's what she told you? Or that the Saturday night "sleepover" at Beth's won't actually include a keg and fifty of Beth's closest friends? How much should you trust, and how much should you verify?

The answer, as usual, depends on your teen: his age, maturity level, temperament, and history of behavior. If you have an open, communicative relationship, you likely already have a gut feeling about maturity, as well as how likely your teen is to respond to peer pressure or to follow rules.

Remember, your teen is on the way to adulthood and deserves to be treated with respect. But "on the way" is the key phrase. As most teens are painfully aware, they're not yet adults and, therefore, require supervision. Generally speaking, younger teens will need more monitoring and should be given less independence than older teens. Just how much monitoring and how much independence is up to you. But there are some general guidelines to follow when thinking about supervising your teen. We recommend, at a minimum, that you:

Know your teen's friends. You can't know what your teen is doing every minute, but getting to know her friends is a good way to get a feel for the influences at play. Invite them over—have your teen host pizza night or a video game competition or some other social activity. Then spend some time getting to know them (but don't make it an inquisition and don't outstay your welcome. They're here for teen time, so set a limit for your involvement and then slip away).

Set the expectation that you'll check up. If you establish this as a given early on, you'll have the least resistance, but if you haven't, it's not too late. You can present your "checking up" as a necessary part of the additional privileges teens get as they mature. So you might say, "You've earned the right to spend more time away from home, and it's fine for you to sleep over at Kelly's, but I need to check in with her mom first." Then be sure to do it. Your teen will likely never admit it, but this can actually have the added benefit of providing a tool to use against peer pressure ("I'm not allowed to go to that party, and my mom will find out if I do. She always calls ahead.").

Be home. If you have to work, as many parents do, you can't be in the home keeping a watchful eye on your teen all the time. But chances are you can be there enough to send a message of awareness. If you're normally not home from work until 6:00, make an effort to alter your schedule from time to time. Drop by in the afternoon, just to check in. And that long weekend away you've been planning? If you have a teen in the house—even one you think is responsible and mature—you'll provide an almost unbearable temptation. You could take your teen along, arrange a stay at a friend's house whose family you trust, or arrange for someone to stay with your teen. We know it's an inconvenience, and when your teen is standing in front of you earnestly professing his maturity and responsibility, it's easy to give in. But by simply removing temptation, you've gone a long way toward helping your teen avoid potentially harmful situations.

Respond fairly, but firmly. We all know that consistency is the key to discipline. It's been true since your teen was a baby, and it's still true today. If you establish a rule and your teen breaks it, you must respond with a reasonable consequence—every time. But be fair; the punishment should fit the crime. Stay calm and keep anger out of your voice. If you can't do that, wait until you've cooled down to decide on a consequence (but don't wait too long—consequences should be fairly immediate).

Be an example. Talk about your values and then demonstrate your commitment to them. If you're a single parent and you tell your teen you don't believe in sex before marriage, live your life accordingly. If you want your teen to be honest with you, then be honest yourself. After all, you're modeling the behavior you want to see emulated.

Accept conflict. Remember the days when your teen was little and you were the hero? She clamored for time with you and, apart from the occasional temper tantrum, accepted your authority as absolute? As you might have already noticed, those days are numbered, thanks to a combination of your teen's improved intellect (they eventually figure out you're not perfect) and increasing desire for independence. While it's tempting to hang on to some of that adoration by slipping into best-friend mode, you won't do your teen any favors by doing so. Teens need a parent rather than a pal. This means there will most likely be conflict as your teen bristles against the restrictions you impose or squirms under the scrutiny of parental supervision. Be respectful, calm, and consistent, and you'll have the best chance of weathering the storm. If you avoid conflict by nature, you might need help, either in setting boundaries or in dealing with the conflict that results. If you had a conflicted relationship with your own parents, you may not have a good model on which to build your own parenting behavior. A good book (see our resources section) or a family counselor or therapist can help guide you in how to set and enforce rules and can also work with your family in resolving conflict. If you feel conflict is seriously affecting your teen's social, school, and home life, you may need the help of a qualified professional. See our sidebar "When Conflict Crosses the Line" on page 207 to learn more.

Find healthy alternatives. One way to make sure your teen is spending time in environments you feel are safe is to steer her toward them. Start young and encourage participation in organized activities with groups that are appropriately supervised. That might mean a church group, but it could also mean a local theater club, organized sports, a volunteer organization, or other outlet. Having more than one social group gives teens options should their relationship with one group take a nosedive. Keep in mind, though, that organized groups aren't babysitters, nor are they vetting the other people who participate. It's still your job to be a part of your teen's life and know what she is doing and with whom.

When Do Teens Have Sex?

Although many parents assume the hours after school and before the end of the typical workday are prime time for teen sex, there's evidence that may not be the case.

One six-year study of 106 fourteen- to eighteen-year-olds by the Indiana University School of Adolescent Medicine found that teens were twice as likely to have sex in the evenings than in the after-school hours.[67] Weekend evenings were the most common time of all. While parental supervision was tied to decreased sexual activity in the afternoon, it wasn't linked to less sex in the evening. Similarly, while skipping school was tied to an increased likelihood of afternoon sex, it didn't impact evening sex.

Teen sexual activity is complex and tied to much more than simply being unsupervised, the study's authors concluded. Other factors, such as time spent with a partner, an argument with a partner (which increased the likelihood of afternoon sex by 60 percent), mood, and having had sexual encounters in the past week all had an impact on whether or not a teen had sex at any given time.

You might take comfort in one of the study's findings, though: The teens studied reported that sex was fairly infrequent, occurring on just 12 percent of the days tracked.

FAIR GAME? RULES YOU CAN MAKE, AND THOSE YOU CAN'T

There is no rulebook for parenting teens, no set of do-this-and-succeed guidelines every family can follow. Since every teen is different, having navigated these waters before doesn't automatically qualify you as an expert, either.

Still, there are some general guidelines you can follow. First, when it comes to teens, there are a few things you shouldn't even attempt to dictate. They are: who teens' friends are; who teens date; and how teens express themselves.

Banning friendships, romantic partners, or creative expressions—such as that Mohawk you love to hate—almost always results in a power struggle and can actually end up encouraging the behavior you object to. Remember that the teenage years are a time of trying on new identities. She may decide she loves the Goth look and stick with it for the rest of her life. But she may also decide in a few months (or years) that pink is the new black and go for an entirely new look. Or that the tongue piercing she longed for isn't getting the reaction she anticipated. Let your teen experiment, especially when there's no clear-cut safety concern.

When you *are* establishing rules, the ideal is to give teens enough leeway to make decisions and learn from mistakes—and also enjoy life—while still keeping them safe and out of situations that might require better judgment or decision making than they possess.

Expect to negotiate as your teen advances through adolescence. Take the curfew you've had in place for the past six months: A time will come when your teen asks to break it, either permanently or for a special occasion. Maybe your teen is ready for the increased responsibility, maybe not. As you negotiate, keep your ultimate goal of safety in mind, as well as the key points you're willing to bend on, but consider, too, a teen's growing need for independence.

That said, we'll get to the areas that relate to sexual activity where you *should* consider providing structure in the form of rules. Some that we recommend:

Where a teen sleeps. You may stipulate that a teen can't sleep at a girlfriend or boyfriend's house, or that your teen must sleep at home. Keep in mind, though, that instituting a lock-down policy—forbidding a teen from sleeping at friends' houses altogether—may backfire in the long run. Instead, establish the expectation of honesty (that teens are going where they say they're going), know their friends, make it a policy to check up, and then enforce the rules consistently.

What goes on in the family's house. It's okay to set boundaries about acceptable behaviors in your home. If you don't want your teen to have sex in your house, that's a valid rule. If you don't want people of the opposite sex in bedrooms, that's reasonable, too. However, it helps if you can explain why. It might be "I'm not comfortable with you having sex here," or "I don't want your little brother to be exposed to that." In addition, it's fair to set rules and enforce them about activities that may be tied to sex, such as the use of alcohol or drugs. Both are illegal for teens to use and also can lower inhibition—two great reasons to restrict their use.

How teens present themselves to the world. This one has many shades of gray and varies by age. We don't recommend that you get into power struggles over your teen's desire to express himself by getting that third ear piercing or trying a new hair color each week. Nor do we recommend going to war over issues of expression if your chief concern is how other people will perceive *you* (as a bad parent, for example). But it is acceptable to establish family standards for clothing you feel is inappropriate for a teen of a certain age and to limit expressions that can't easily be undone (that rose tattoo on your teen's shoulder, for example). This is a balancing act; a fight over a midriff-baring tank top can easily escalate into a full-blown power struggle (and even if you win, your teenage daughter might just change, slip the offending shirt into her bag, and put it on the minute she's out of your reach).

The struggle may be worth it, depending on her age, if you think the top sends an inappropriately sexualized image (and therefore might bring on a type of attention your teen is not ready to handle). And then again, it might not. Think about what's most important to you and then focus your efforts on those issues. You might hate that he insists on wearing ripped jeans and a shirt that looks like it came from the bottom of the hamper, but since the risks of such attire are minimal, you might leave that decision to your teen. However, you might decide to ban clothing with profanity, body piercings, or clothing that is extremely provocative (keeping in mind that your sense of provocative might not be the same as your teen's).

You also can use the fact that in most states you need permission to get a tattoo if you're under eighteen (although if he does decide to get one when he turns eighteen, make sure you've talked to him about only using a qualified tattoo artist who uses sterilized equipment, because dirty needles can be a source of HIV infection).

Whatever you decide, present it to your teen in a calm, reasonable tone. Ideally, this should be done before she comes home from the mall with a raunchy T-shirt or tries to dash out the door in four-inch heels and a mini-dress the size of a cocktail napkin. If you're having a general "rules of the house" sit-down, you can bring it up then, or you can use an everyday event or example in pop culture to start the conversation.

One Way to Say It ...

Fifteen-year-old Heidi has a good relationship with her parents. She is responsible and mature and generally complies with rules at home and school. However, her parents have noticed that her friends have started to dress in a way that seems too adult. So far, Heidi hasn't pushed the envelope, and her parents feel pretty sure she won't do anything drastic. Still, they've decided to talk about the rules and responsibilities of appearance. Although the family's schedule makes family dinners less frequent than Heidi's parents would like, they make an effort to sit down to a meal together at least three times a week. Heidi's father uses one of these occasions to open a conversation on the topic.

Dad:
> You know, I was in line at the mall behind this girl who had places of her face pierced that I didn't even know you *could* pierce.

Heidi:
> Ha, ha, Dad.

Dad:
> Okay, I know. But it did make me realize that we've never really talked about what's okay to wear and what's not.

Heidi:
> I'm not getting a nose ring, Dad!

Dad:

Well, that's good news. But since we're all together right now, this is probably a good time to talk about this sort of thing. Mom and I know you're responsible, and we're really proud of you. And we're not about to tell you what to do with your hair or what color shirt to wear.

Heidi:

Thank God.

Dad:

We want you to look as beautiful, smart, and level-headed as we know you are, but if you decide a crew cut is "the true you" or that wrinkles in your clothes are "in," we're not going to stop you. You have a right to choose for yourself. But you also have some responsibilities, in the form of following some basic rules. There are just a few things about how you look that are really important to us.

Heidi:

Okay, I have a feeling I'm not going to like this.

Dad:

Maybe not, but we're really trying to give you room to be you, without going too far out of the family's comfort zone. Mainly, we think a lot of the clothing that's marketed to kids your age is just inappropriate. There's a lot of stuff that teenagers might not find offensive but that most other people would, and other clothing is too grown up for someone your age. So, it's not okay to wear clothing that would offend most people. That means no swear words or offensive symbols.

Heidi:

That's fine. I think stuff like that is dumb anyhow.

Dad:

Great. Also, we think you should wear clothes that are appropriate for your age. Tops that are very low cut or skirts that are really short are likely to bring you attention that may be hard to handle. We're not going to take a ruler to your skirts, but generally if it's shorter than mid-thigh, it's not okay to wear. And for tops, you'll have to use your best judgment in deciding whether it's too revealing. If you think Mom or I would be upset if you wore something, or think it's "too sexy," you should ask whether it's okay before you wear it out of the house. All right?

Heidi:

Dad, everyone wears short skirts. You're going to make me dress like a loser.

Dad:

No, I promise we're not. I'm talking about clothing that's on the extreme end. We're really not going to step in and dictate fashion. There are plenty of clothes that don't cross the line and are appropriate for a fifteen-year-old. When you're older, you can decide for yourself whether you're comfortable with the attention grown-up clothing brings.

Heidi:

All right. I'm sure those prairie dresses will look good with my belly button ring.

Dad:

Very funny. Actually, getting pierced or tattooed is the only other rule. Tattoos are permanent and there's a safety risk, so they're out until you're eighteen. Then you can decide for yourself. We're not totally against piercings, but they do require our permission.

It depends on where and on how old you are when you get it, so just ask us and we'll consider it.

Heidi:

Well, I don't have any plans right now so you're lucky.

Dad:

We definitely are lucky to have you, Heidi.

Keep in mind that if you're the one with the cash or paying the credit card bill, you're in a position of influence (you can refuse to buy your fourteen-year-old thong underwear, for example). That's helpful with younger teens, although as your teen gets older and more financially independent, the balance of power will shift. You'll still need to make and enforce rules, but you'll have to accept that some negotiation may be necessary. Again, focus on what's truly important to you and give your teen room to grow.

Explain the Rules

It may sound obvious, but you can't expect anyone to follow a rule unless you discuss it first. To do that, you need to think about which behaviors you want to regulate and how important compliance is for each. Take a few minutes now to jot down behaviors that are most important to you. Remember to focus on safety, which you can regulate, rather than on values, which you can't.

The dinner table can be a great setting for family discussions, so talking about rules over a meal is usually a good plan. But you can also call a family meeting or simply ask your teen to sit down for a chat. When you do, be sure to:

Start small. Rather than coming up with a list of rules as long as your arm (your teen will mentally "check out" after rule four or five), select a few to talk about. If sexual activity is your chief concern right now, focus on the rules surrounding that. They might include where your teen can sleep, appropriate behavior in the house when with someone of the opposite sex, curfews, online activity, or other topics that concern you.

Give it a positive spin. Instead of "laying down the law," you may want to present the talk as "discussing privileges and responsibilities." It's spin, to be sure, and your teen won't be totally fooled, but starting with a negative is sure to put him on the defensive.

Discuss Privileges. How much freedom your teen has will depend on a variety of factors, including age, maturity level, history of behavior, and family comfort level. For younger teens, privileges might include being able to go to same-sex sleepovers or out on dates. For older teens, privileges likely will include staying out later and having more freedom in where they go and with whom they spend time. Related privileges might include use of the car, allowance, and nonfamily vacations, outings, or events.

Discuss Responsibilities. These are otherwise known as "the rules." Be specific about your expectations and explain why each rule is important. Frame it as a responsibility. For example: "You're old enough now to go to the movies with your friends on the weekend, but it's your responsibility to be back by 10 p.m." Stick with the authoritative model but negotiate the specifics, if necessary. The only caveat is that you'll need to take your teen's temperament into account. If your teen is more likely to respond to a "rule" than a responsibility, then we recommend sticking with the term *rule*.

Discuss Consequences. You don't have do this every time your teen walks out the door—sending someone off every Friday night with, "Be back by curfew or you're not going anywhere tomorrow night" isn't likely to be effective. But since you're talking about privileges and responsibilities, it makes sense to establish the likely consequences for rule breaking. When you do, remember to:

- **Tie privileges to consequences.** For example, "If you miss your curfew, you'll lose the use of the car for the weekend," or, "If you're not home by 10 p.m., you'll have to stay home Friday night."
- **Be specific.** Vague demands such as "Don't do anything to embarrass me," or "I don't want you staying out until all hours of the night" aren't effective. Instead, define what you mean. Some examples:
    - "Your curfew is midnight on weekends and 10 p.m. on weeknights."
    - "People of the opposite sex aren't allowed in bedrooms in our house."
    - "I don't think sex is appropriate for people your age, so I don't want you to have sex here in the house, whether I'm home or not."

Consider temperament and history. An adolescent who is impulsive, or who has had a hard time following rules since childhood, is not likely to suddenly morph into a by-the-book teen (although if your teen does, you should do a few cartwheels— there's reason to celebrate). If your teen complies with your requests less than half the time or is routinely rude or disrespectful to you, you will likely need to provide more supervision in the form of stricter rules than you might with a naturally compliant teen. Keep in mind that no one is perfect. Your teen will likely have slip-ups (some teens more so than others).

Notice good behavior. You can and should encourage rule following by rewarding good behavior. You don't have to tell your teen you're doing this. (Although you might consider using the point reward system Gerald R. Patterson and Marion S. Forgatch lay out in their book, *Parents and Adolescents Living Together*. In this system you *do* tell teens you're rewarding good behavior.)

When teens follow the rules, offer praise. Hugs and smiles work wonders, too. And, of course, you might want to pony up some more tangible pats-on-the-back by surprising your teen with tickets to the movies, a new video game, a gift card for a favorite store, or whatever you think might get the biggest "woo-hoo!" from your teen. Don't forget that spending time together—whether it's a trip to the mall, a bike ride, or some other activity—is a way of building good will you can draw on when you need to be firm about the rules.

Teen Targeted: Appropriate Rules

Under 15: Teens this age are new to many of the social situations they'll encounter. Curfews, restrictions on online activities, and limits on certain activities at home are in order. We'd recommend:

- **Curfews:** You might have to make exceptions depending on a teen's extracurricular activities, but most teens this age should be home no later than 8 p.m. on a school night. On weekends, 10 p.m. is reasonable, although you should also be aware of where your teen is, and with whom. Remind your teen that curfews are a way to teach rule or law abidance (they'll need that throughout life) and to earn trust and privileges. They're also, of course, a way to help make sure teens stay safe.
- **Online restrictions:** Talk to your teen about appropriate online behavior and which sites are off-limits (you can also buy software that limits access and use the family filter on some search engines, but you should talk to your teen about it, too, since such filters aren't foolproof and won't be on every computer your teen

uses). Some suggestions: Any site marked "XXX" or that requires you to say you're eighteen or older is off-limits, as is any site that portrays pornography or adult sexual activity. If your teen accidentally goes to an adult site, she should tell you immediately. You might also suggest a few teen-oriented sites your teen can go to for answers to questions about the human body or sexuality (see the back of this book for our picks, and see a discussion of Rules for the Wired World on page 208).

- **Behavior at home:** We're sure you have lots of rules about behavior already (no shoes on the couch, dirty clothes go in the hamper, etc.), but there are a few you might consider that are related to sexuality. You'll have to determine for yourself which limitations fit your family, but for this age group, you might consider: no members of the opposite sex in bedrooms; no members of the opposite sex allowed in the house when parents aren't home; no guests in the home without the parents being aware of their presence; and no closed doors if you're in a room with a member of the opposite sex.

15 to 17: During these years, your teen will be eager to negotiate the rules, and you'll need to give a little. As your teen gets closer to seventeen, consider extending curfews, relaxing limits on online activities, and possibly loosening limits on behaviors in the home (although it's possible that these will remain relatively static for as long as your teen lives in your home).

- **Curfews:** Teens at the younger end of this age group would have many more restrictions than older teens. For fifteen-year-olds, a weeknight curfew of 8 p.m. and weekend curfew of 10 p.m. makes sense (you can also ask other parents to see what the norms are in your community). For sixteen-year-olds you might increase it slightly, and for seventeen-year-olds, a later curfew makes sense—perhaps 10 p.m. on weeknights and midnight or 1 a.m. on weekends.
- **Online restrictions:** If you haven't already, you should talk to teens of any age about Internet safety. For fifteen- and sixteen-year-olds, software and filters still make sense, as does avoiding any site that requires you to state that you're over eighteen or deals in adult material. Seventeen-year-olds are probably ready to tackle the Web unhindered, and although you can suggest that they avoid adult sites—they're not yet 18 so those adult sites are still off limits—if they want to surf for porn, they're probably going to find a way to do it.
- **Behavior at home:** You may want to allow your teen more leeway in this area, depending on your views and values.

18 and Over: If your teen is over eighteen but still in high school, you'll have to balance his or her right to independence with practical matters, such as getting enough sleep on school nights and maintaining order at home. But for the most part, once your teen turns eighteen, it's time to let go and trust.

One Way to Say It ...

Sixteen-year-old Cara and her parents have a healthy relationship. They have talked over the years about their values, the rules of the house, and the consequences of breaking rules. Cara has been seeing Brian for six months, and the two seem to be getting serious. Cara's parents recently revisited the topic of STIs and birth control with Cara and reminded her that they thought she should wait until she's out of high school to have sex. They also told her that if she did have sex, she should protect herself from pregnancy and STIs. At the end of the conversation, they talked about the rules of the house.

Mom:

> We know you're responsible, and we're really proud of you for always being home before your curfew. But now that you're in a serious relationship, we do have a few other responsibilities that we should talk about.

Cara:

> Okay, like what?

Mom:

> Well, first, it's fine for Brian to come over and spend time with you, but bedrooms are off-limits. If you're going to spend time with him here, you should do that in the family room or the other common areas. That means no sleeping over, and it means keeping things relatively cool while you're in the house.

Cara:

> Mom, I'm not going to have sex with him in the next room! God, that's so gross.

Mom:

I know you're not. But that brings up a good point. We have to keep your brother in mind, too. He's younger, and there are certain things I don't think he needs to be exposed to yet. That means that even when Dad and I aren't here, we really need you and Brian to be mindful of the rules and respectful of our wishes. Does that make sense?

Cara:

Yeah, that makes sense. I'm not going to corrupt the family, Mom.

Mom:

Well, that's good to hear (smiling). I don't think you're corrupt anyhow, sweetie. Okay, so there are a few other responsibilities we should talk about ...

THE ENFORCER: WHAT TO DO WHEN TEENS BREAK RULES

You've established the rules and communicated the consequences. Your teen nodded, sincerely promised to abide and then, oops, stayed out past curfew last night. What's a parent to do? That depends on your family dynamic, your teen's history of rule following (or not), and the circumstances of the situation. But there are some guidelines to follow when a rule has been broken.

Don't let little slips slide. It's easy to slip into the permissive parent zone when confronted with minor violations. After all, conflict is unpleasant and time-consuming. Does it really matter if your teen comes home half an hour after her curfew? Or if she said she was at Lisa's but actually went to Lori's without telling you? The answer is, if it breaks the rules, then, yes, it's important. Ignoring small slip-ups and then "getting tough" when a teen really pulls a doozy isn't effective parenting. Small violations should be consistently met with small consequences. So, coming home after curfew would result in an immediate (but relatively small) loss of a privilege, such as the right to go out the following night or an earlier curfew for a week.

Set a respectful tone. Sarcasm or snide comments are likely to result in a similar response from your teen. You snarl, and your teen snarls back. If, on the other hand, you address your teen calmly and with respect, you'll have a much better chance of having a constructive conversation. This isn't easy, we know. Count to ten (silently), take a few deep breaths, recite the alphabet, do whatever you can to put yourself in a calmer state before you talk to your teen. And if you can't …

Set a time to talk. As we mentioned in chapter 2, there are good times to talk and not so good times to talk. Keep in mind, however, that consequences should be fairly immediate. The sooner you can calm down and address the situation, the better.

Identify the broken rule. Exactly which rule was broken might be obvious, but it's possible that it's not. Meeting your teen at the door with, "You're grounded for a week!" isn't the best approach. Instead, calmly explain what you believe your teen did wrong.

Get the facts. Ask what happened. Your teen will likely have a reason for breaking the rules (whether it's a valid reason is another story entirely). Give her a chance to speak—and listen.

Be clear about the consequences for breaking rules.
Effective consequences are those that are:

- Limited in scope: Instead of throwing the book at your teen, so to speak, pick one consequence. It might be "No use of the car for the weekend," rather than "You can't talk to your friends or use the car or go out." If there are mitigating circumstances, there's room for negotiation.

- Defined in duration: Try, "You're not allowed to go out socially for the next two weekends," rather than just, "You're grounded."
- Enforceable: Make sure you'll be available, willing, and able to enforce whatever punishment you establish. If you're not home after school, don't go with "no TV after school." If your teen needs the car to get to work, school, therapy, or some other worthy cause, don't say "no using the car" (although you can say "no using the car except to drive to …").
- Fair: Consequences should match the degree of the rule broken. In other words, the punishment should fit the crime.
- Productive, if possible: One option is to create consequences that result in something positive and concrete being accomplished. Some examples might be weeding the garden together, cleaning the car, or volunteering. It's better still if you can do it together (but if you do, make sure you do it cheerfully. It's a consequence, not torture.).

Wipe the slate clean. Once your teen has completed the task or consequence, start over. The only time you discuss past rule breaking is if there seems to be a pattern of disobeying, in which case you might say, "This seems to be becoming a bad habit" and then discuss how the "habit" can be broken.

Although you may want to increase the penalty for a repeat violation, don't fall into the trap of ever-greater escalations. At some point, they'll become impossible to enforce. If your teen ignores the punishment or continues to flaunt the rules, you should seek help, either through a family counselor or a good book (we recommend *Parents and Adolescents Living Together* by Gerald Patterson and Marion S. Forgatch).

Ashley's Story

Ashley was a seventeen-year-old high school senior when she started dating twenty-four-year-old Nate, whom she met through an online community dedicated to anime, an art style she loved. Nate was employed, living on his own, and hung out with a crowd that seemed sophisticated to Ashley.

Ashley's parents, Cliff and Mona, had told Ashley over the years about their values: They didn't believe in sex before marriage. They felt that Ashley shared their values but were alarmed when they discovered Nate's age. Nate, they thought, might pressure her to be more of an adult than she really was. Whenever Ashley mentioned him, her mother made a face and told her, "He's too old for you. I really don't like you seeing him." Although she didn't forbid Ashley from seeing Nate, Mona made it clear that Nate wasn't welcome in the home.

Ashley had a curfew of midnight on weekends, but Nate often kept her out after curfew. When Ashley's parents confronted her, she complained that the curfew was impossible to keep since she, Nate, and his friends often dined late (and long). Ashley explained that she felt bad dragging Nate away from his friends and embarrassed to be the "little kid" who had to get home by midnight. Ashley's parents told her they wouldn't budge on the curfew, but they usually let her off with a stern warning that "there would be consequences" if she didn't start following the curfew.

As the months went on, Ashley continued to abuse her curfew, and Mona's objections increased. She found herself getting angry—and letting it show—whenever Nate's name was mentioned. Ashley, in response, became increasingly defensive.

When Ashley graduated from high school, Nate suggested a weekend trip away. Ashley's parents objected, saying that until she turned eighteen they didn't want her vacationing with her boyfriend. Ashley pouted, shouted, and then went anyway. When she returned, her father confronted her and angrily told her she was grounded for a month and could have no contact with Nate during that time. Ashley argued that she was old enough to make her own decisions. Her father shot back with "As long as you're under my roof, you'll follow my rules."

Ashley, feeling disrespected and forced to choose between her parents and Nate, chose to move in with Nate. Ashley's parents were devastated but also extremely angry with their daughter. They had minimal contact with her for several months. Over the next year Ashley decided that she and Nate weren't right for each other after all. She moved out, and he moved on. Eventually her relationship with her parents improved, although it took many years before they were all able to fully forgive each other.

Most parents can relate to Cliff and Mona's dismay. They had a valid reason to view the relationship with caution. But their combination of permissive and authoritarian parenting proved damaging to their relationship with their daughter, as well as ineffective. Instead, an authoritative approach likely would have helped. Some guidelines they could have followed:

Enforcing rules: Breaking curfew comes with a consequence, every time. By letting Ashley off the hook when she missed curfew, her parents sent the message that the rules wouldn't be enforced and set the stage for a major blow-up later, when she violated a "bigger" rule.

Negotiating: The reality of Ashley's relationship was that she was dating an adult, which meant her parents would either have to relax the curfew or be creative in helping her follow the rules. They might have worked with Ashley to help her get home on her own (even if Nate wasn't ready to leave), either by giving Ashley the family car on weekend nights, or at the very least talking to her about always having cab fare and a cell phone on hand. This would have given her more control over getting home—and fewer excuses. Her parents might also have role-played ways that Ashley could gracefully leave a social situation without calling attention to her age.

Being nonjudgmental: Mona decided early on that she didn't like Nate due to his age, and she let Ashley know it every chance she got. Instead, she could have talked to Ashley in a nonjudgmental voice about the risks of dating someone who is older. In addition, if Cliff and Mona had made an effort to get to know Nate—by spending time with Ashley and Nate instead of banning him from the house—they would have gained credibility with Ashley and insight into the relationship. They might even have found that they liked him and that he didn't pose the threat they were so worried about.

Sharing values, but respecting rights: Cliff and Mona were right to tell Ashley how they felt about teens and sex. But they also should have recognized that, at seventeen, Ashley was old enough to decide for herself whether to be sexually active (and with whom). With that in mind, they could have talked to her about STIs and birth control and encouraged her to see an adolescent medicine specialist for more information. They might have suggested she put off the weekend away until she and Nate had had a pre-sex talk and each had seen a doctor.

The Wrong (and Right) Way to Say It ...

Consider the two examples outlined below, in which we dissect two conversations. Both are responses to the same situation: A teen has broken the rules by letting her boyfriend sneak into her bedroom. In both, the mother catches the boyfriend leaving the house at 4 a.m. and confronts her daughter.

What not to say ...

Mom:

(raising her voice) Lindsay, I can't believe you had Brad in your room. What were you doing? How could you sneak around like that? That's so slutty. And what will the neighbors say when they see him leaving the house at the crack of dawn?

[*What's wrong: Mom makes several mistakes here, letting her anger take over (by yelling, calling names, and then posing rapid-fire questions) and referencing the neighbors. She should have stayed calm and focused on the teen, not the neighbors.*]

Lindsay:

We weren't doing anything, I swear.

Mom:

You're lying. I know you two were fooling around.

[*What's wrong: Instead of listening to her daughter to find out what happened, Mom goes right to an accusation.*]

Lindsay:

Why should I even talk to you when you never listen to what I say? I hate living here.

Mom:

> Too bad. You're stuck here. And you're grounded. Don't even think about leaving this house until I say so.

[*What's wrong: Mom completely ignores her daughter's complaint and then, without waiting for her own temper to cool, makes a decree that is both unenforceable and undefined.*]

Try this instead ...

Mom:

> Lindsay, I'm really upset. We've already talked about the fact that boys aren't allowed in your bedroom, and about treating each other with respect by being honest. Having Brad in your room breaks both of those rules.

[*What's right: Mom acknowledges her feelings and identifies the rule that was broken.*]

Lindsay:

> Mom, I know I shouldn't have, but it's not what you think.

Mom:

> All right, I'm listening. Why don't you tell me what was going on?

[*What's right: Mom gives her daughter the chance to explain.*]

Lindsay:

> Well, Brad got in a big fight with his dad and he stormed out. He couldn't go home right away. He was just really mad and upset, and he needed to talk. I didn't know what else to do. I couldn't leave him outside in the cold.

Mom:

> Well, now that you have a minute to think about it, what might have been a better option?

[What's right: Mom listens and then helps Lindsay understand how she could have handled it better.]

Lindsay:

> Um, I guess I could have woken you up and asked. But you have to work tomorrow. You would have killed me, and you know it.

Mom:

> You know what, Lindsay, I don't think I would have. I know how you feel about Brad. Yes, I get cranky when I don't get a good night's sleep. But if you feel like you need to help your friend, then I think I would understand that. And it's certainly better than having you sneak around.

Lindsay:

> Okay, I guess I get that. I won't do it again, I swear.

Mom:

> Good. I understand why you did it, but we still have to respect each other and the rules of the house. So, I want you to cancel any plans you have for Friday and Saturday night and stay home instead. This way Brad "gets it," too. Let's talk with your dad and discuss whether or not it is okay for Brad to stay over in the

future if things are bad at his house. If we decide that's okay, he can sleep on the couch, but not in your room.

[*What's right: Mom is consistent in enforcing the rules, despite Lindsay's excuse. She also establishes a reasonable consequence that fits the violation, while still showing trust and concern about Brad. Since Lindsay now has to cancel her plans for Friday and Saturday, Mom could plan a family outing/trip for the weekend (for example, go to a movie together or for a hike). That sends the message that Mom still loves Lindsay, but she has to follow the rules.*]

SHE CANNOT TELL A LIE? WELL, NOT EXACTLY ...

Not all teens lie. But the teen years are likely to include times when even normally honest people feel compelled to be dishonest. Sometimes we lie to cover up a mistake, sometimes to do something we want to do (but know we're not supposed to), and sometimes it's to avoid a conflict.

Sometimes teens find themselves trapped in a web of lies, telling one to cover for the last, and digging themselves deeper into a hole of dishonesty they never intended to create. Remember, teens lack experience and are still figuring out, sometimes by trial and error, how human relationships work.

Whatever the reason, lying isn't uncommon. In one study of 281 college students, the vast majority admitted to having lied to their parents during high school, and 49 percent reported having lied about their sexual behavior (only one topic was more common: About 65 percent of students admitted to lying about "where I was"). Women lied more frequently than men about their sexual behavior, and the opposite-sex parent was lied to more often than the same-sex parent. Still, 85 percent of respondents said they were still "basically honest" people, and nearly 75 percent said that as they got older, their lying decreased.[68]

So just because your teen lies on occasion doesn't mean he or she is going to grow into a dishonest adult. But because trust is a crucial part of any healthy relationship, and research shows that frequent lying does damage to the parent-child bond, lying does require that you take immediate and consistent action.

If you've discovered your teen is lying, or suspect it to be the case, your response should be similar to any other rule breaking. In general, you should:

Keep your anger in check. It might hurt to think that your teen has deceived you, but an angry outburst isn't going to help. Remember that you don't know all the facts yet.

Get the facts. Ask your teen exactly what happened. You might get a confession, but it's also possible that your teen will continue to lie, hoping that you'll eventually be convinced. If you strongly suspect lying, say so, and explain why it's important that you know the truth. You might cite safety reasons or the fact that you need to know the truth so that you can reestablish trust. After all, you can't have a relationship of mutual respect if you don't have trust.

Try to understand why. Ask why your teen felt the need to lie. She might say something that gives you insight into something you need to change. For example, if your teen lied because she feels that you've been dishonest with her, you may have a deeper issue to work on. If the motivation behind lying was to deliberately hurt others, you'll need to find out why to make sure it doesn't become a pattern in adulthood.

Remember the authoritative parent. Set high expectations in honesty as in other things. "I really expect you to be honest with me," is one way to say it. Tie the expectation to the privileges the teen enjoys. If the expectation isn't met, take away privileges.

Praise honesty. If your teen is coming clean, thank him for telling you the truth. Acknowledge that sometimes telling the truth is hard and being honest takes courage. Repeat that trust is a critical part of your relationship and that being truthful now is helping to restore your trust.

Minimize excuses. You should listen, but you don't have to accept any excuses for lying. In fact, you should meet such excuses with a firm, "I understand what you're saying, but there's no good reason for you to lie to me."

Be fair. How you respond depends on the circumstances and on your relationship with your teen. If the lie's purpose was to hide another violation—say, going to a party your teen wasn't allowed to attend—your consequence for the first rule breaking may be enough (and should follow the guidelines outlined on page 198). If your teen lied to avoid disappointing you (telling you she was a virgin when she wasn't), no consequences may be necessary. In that case, it's more effective to focus on creating an environment where your teen feels safe telling you something, even if it is likely to disappoint you.

When Conflict Crosses the Line: What to Do with a Troubled Teen

It's normal for children to buck the system occasionally and for conflict to be a part of their relationship with parents. But truly rebellious behavior in adolescence is cause for concern.

If your teen is frequently uncooperative or openly hostile to the point that it disrupts life at school, among friends, and at home, you may have a bigger problem on your hands, and one that requires the help of a mental health professional.

The root cause of such behavior can vary. Somewhere between 5 and 15 percent of teens suffer from oppositional defiant disorder (ODD), according to the American Association of Child Psychiatrists (AACAP). Symptoms, according to AACAP, can include frequent temper tantrums, excessive arguing with adults, active defiance and refusal to comply with adult requests and rules, deliberate attempts to annoy or upset people, blaming others for mistakes or misbehavior, being easily annoyed by others, frequent anger and resentment, mean and hateful talking when upset, and seeking revenge.

Other disorders can cause similar behaviors, however, so evaluation by a qualified mental health professional is in order. In addition, children and teens with ODD can go on to develop conduct disorder, a more serious condition that includes a set of behavioral and emotional problems ranging from aggression to lying, stealing, and other dangerous behaviors. Again, the help of a qualified professional is vital in such cases.

RULES FOR THE WIRED WORLD: KEEPING YOUR TEEN SAFE ONLINE

To parents, the Internet can seem a terrifying place. It offers up easy access to adult material—some relatively harmless, some that is inappropriate even for most adults—with almost complete anonymity. In addition, it can easily be misused by anyone seeking to exploit a young person.

But the Internet is an indelible part of teens' lives. It is highly unlikely you could keep your teen away even if you tried. And would you really want to? Despite its foibles, the Internet can be a boon for teens, linking them to boundless educational information, connecting them with others who have similar interests or concerns, and giving them a fast and efficient outlet for communicating with friends.

Still, it's a good idea to put safety measures in place. If you're concerned about pornography, there are software programs that can restrict access to certain sites, and some search engines offer family filters (Google's is called SafeSearch, and it screens out most adult content). Keep in mind, though, that no software is perfect, so you shouldn't rely solely on software to keep your teen safe online. (We'll give you more pointers in a moment.)

For many parents, even scarier than the idea of their teen surfing for porn is the danger posed by online predators. The perception may be that predators strike by pretending to be a peer and then forcibly assaulting young children, but Internet-initiated sex crimes are often far more insidious.[69]

In fact, most sex offenders who initiate sex crimes online don't hide the fact that they're adults, and only a small fraction ever resort to force. Instead, sex offenders typically spend time "grooming" victims, making efforts to gain their trust and then seducing them into sexual relationships. Predators bank on the appeal of romance or sexual adventure, or both.

The good news is that while some behaviors clearly increase a teen's risk of falling victim to an online predator, merely being online doesn't. In fact, using popular social networking sites such as MySpace and Facebook isn't linked to increased risk, according to research.

What does put teens at risk is engaging in risky online behaviors, such as maintaining buddy lists that include strangers, discussing sex online with people they don't know, and being rude or nasty online.

It's important to note that teens with histories of sexual or physical abuse, family problems, and risk taking on- and offline are most at risk of falling victim to online predators. And teens who are gay or questioning their orientation may be more vulnerable than the teen population at large, especially if they haven't come out to their family and friends.

So, how do you keep your teen safe? Setting guidelines for your teen's online use is a good place to start. Here's how to protect your teen online:

- Keep the computer in a high-traffic part of the house where an adult can (and will) glance at the screen periodically.

- Routinely check your browser's history (if you don't know how, get someone to show you) to see which sites your teen has visited. But keep in mind that a computer-savvy teen can erase the history.

- Spend time with your children on the Internet. When you do, steer them to safe sites and talk about Internet safety. Tell teens to avoid sites that are billed as "XXX" or "for 18 and over" and to tell you immediately if they stumble on an inappropriate site or if they view anything that makes them feel uncomfortable or scared. You can also send them to NetSmartz.com (www.netsmartz.org), a website hosted by the National Center for Missing and Exploited Children that is geared toward teaching children and adolescents about Internet safety (www.NetSmartz411.org, meanwhile, offers parents detailed guidelines on keeping their kids safe).

- Help your teen be Web-savvy. Teens should view Web content (and online contact with others) with a critical eye and be aware that not all of what they read or are told by people they meet online is true. You should also tell your teen not to share passwords and to limit personal information posted or distributed online. Finally, teens using social networking sites should know how to use privacy settings so that only people they know can view their information.

- Ask your Internet provider about features that allow parents to block their children's access to adult-oriented sites, "chat rooms," and bulletin boards. And use the family filter on popular search engines.

- Talk frankly to your teen about how sexual predators operate. Explain to your teen that sexual predators don't necessarily abduct small children and forcibly assault them. A sexual predator is more likely to seek out a young person and spend weeks or months developing a relationship with the end goal being sex. The victim may willingly meet the predator and even consent to sex. That doesn't mean it's harmless or isn't a crime (if the teen is below the age of consent). Your teen should be extremely wary of anyone showing either a romantic or deep personal interest if that person is more than four years older.

- Talk to your teen about when it is appropriate to meet face to face with someone they've met online. This isn't the same as dictating who their friends are. Instead, it involves setting guidelines for what to do before you meet anyone in person for the first time (see below).

- Report inappropriate contact. It's illegal to knowingly send unsolicited obscene material to a person under the age of sixteen or to use a misleading domain name to lure a child under sixteen into viewing harmful material (whether or not it's classified as obscene). Report such incidents to the National Center for Missing and Exploited Children, which has a Cyber-Tipline (www.missingkids.com or 800.843.5678). You should also report any suspicious contact to your Internet service provider. If you fear a predator is communicating with your child, you might also want to contact your local authorities (that becomes a must if you feel a predator is trying to lure your teen into a face-to-face meeting).

If He's on the Level, Why Won't He Give Me His Number?

Connecting with others online is part of today's teenage experience. Sometimes they're meeting up with people they know, and sometimes they're making ties with total strangers. Most of the contact is safe; some is not.

Although you want to discourage online dating at this age, you also *should* establish guidelines for teens to follow if they meet someone online, since a meeting may or may not be presented as a "date."

Such guidelines are aimed at making sure your teen isn't being deceived by someone with harmful intentions. Even if that knowledge isn't needed now, it likely will be as your teen reaches adulthood and experiments with online dating. The guidelines are:

Establish that people are who they say they are.
Get the person's full name, telephone number, and as much other identifying information as possible. And then verify as much of what you're told as you can. That means calling the phone number several times and, at the very least, doing a Google search on the person's name. If things don't add up—he said he's twenty but his Match.com profile says he's forty-five, or he said he lives alone but there's a woman's voice on the answering machine—think twice about meeting him in person.

Meet in public and let it be known. If you're going to meet someone you've met online, meet in a public place, such as a coffee shop. And let several people know exactly who you're meeting and when. It's good to also arrange for an "I'm safe" call at a given time. That means you tell another friend you'll call—or arrange for the friend to call you—at an appointed time to say that you're safe.

Don't drink or do drugs. Especially when you're with someone you barely know, it's not a good idea to be under the influence of anything that will dull your reflexes or lower your inhibitions. And don't leave your drink unattended (which leaves you open to the risk of it being tampered with).

Have a phone and cash. Carry a cell phone and enough cash to pay for a cab. Don't accept a ride home from a person you've just met.

Keep the personal details to a minimum. This is a must for any online meeting but should also hold true once you've met in person. Wait until you've met the person several times to reveal your home address or other personal information.

Go with your gut. If you feel like something isn't right or the person isn't being truthful, trust your instincts. End the meeting and get to a safe place.

Consider the Future

There is another risk that may be alien to teens, who, as a whole, have embraced a level of exhibitionism that would make most of their parents squirm with discomfort. To teens, posting the details of their daily lives on social networking sites and blogs is as natural as chatting on the landline was for their parents. But that doesn't mean it's always harmless.

Just as you did when talking to your teen about reputation among friends, it's important to remind your teen that everything they do online is available for the world to see, even years in the future.

College and corporate recruiters routinely check social networking sites and use Google to research potential candidates. So, while it may be fun for your son or daughter to recount that random hookup at last night's party, teens should be aware that it's possible that people beyond their immediate circle of friends—a future boss or in-laws, perhaps—might see it. And if that doesn't seem to matter much now, it may in the very near future.

As scary as it is to think of your teen's every action on public display, should that drive you to police cyberspace, protecting the virtual virtue of your teenager? What if you happen to stumble onto your teen's online networking page? Do you have a right to read it just because it's on the Internet?

The answer isn't as clear-cut as it might seem. Unlike handwritten journals or diaries—which are clearly off-limits, in case you're wondering—online records are, by their very nature, in the public domain. Your teen may have no problem with you "friending" her on her favorite social networking site. And an aboveboard connection like that doesn't likely present a problem. However, we recommend against online snooping or secret check-ups.

If you do stumble across information that you feel indicates a safety risk (or a serious violation of the rules), you should address the issue. Be honest about how you discovered the information. Then talk about what you found.

Keep in mind, too, that it's possible your discovery wasn't a coincidence. A Web page left open or a letter lying where you're bound to see it might be a deliberate attempt by your teen to start a conversation with you. If that's the case, recognize that your teen is seeking your help in the only way he or she knows how. This may mean you'll go a little lighter on the consequences and instead focus more on helping to find a solution.

CHAPTER 8

When It's Not Okay:
Red Flags and Risky Sexual Behavior

You may find the very presence of this chapter alarming. As if STIs, teen pregnancy, and online predators aren't enough, we're throwing more frightening possibilities at you. We know—it's a lot to take in. But we've included it because we want to address potentially serious and harmful behaviors. Before you read on, remember this: Most teens are happy, healthy, and perfectly able to cope with the trials of adolescence.

Still—here it comes—dangers do exist. And even if you've come to accept the reality of your teen's sexual activity and respect teens' right to make their own decisions, there are certain conditions under which you may need to take action to protect your teen.

Some of the situations that might warrant more of a hands-on approach than we've advocated in our earlier chapters are:

- a sexually active child under the age of fourteen
- a sexually active teen aged sixteen or under with a partner who is more than three years older, or an older teen whose partner is four or more years older
- a teen involved with a partner who is physically, emotionally, or verbally abusive
- a teen involved in high-risk sexual activity, such as vaginal or anal intercourse without a condom

- a teen whose sexual activity is combined with drug or alcohol abuse
- a teen who exhibits any of the warning signs of depression
- a teen who harms himself

WHEN AGE IS AN ISSUE

Teens mature at different rates, and the norms of the family and neighborhood may influence the judgment of when it's okay for teens to have sex, but generally, experts agree that sexual activity is inappropriate for anyone under the age of fourteen.

Age also becomes an issue if there's a large age gap between the partners. This is especially true for younger teens. Research has shown that young teens who are sexually active with older partners are at greater risk of pregnancy and STIs. In one study that examined data from 7th through 12th graders, girls who had sex before the age of sixteen with a partner who was at least four years older were twice as likely to test positive for an STI as girls who had sex before sixteen with a similar-aged partner, or older teens who had sex with an older partner.[70] Boys were less likely to have sex before sixteen with an older partner, but those who did were twice as likely to test positive for an STI as boys who delayed sex, regardless of the age of their partner.

Why the increased risk? Relationships with big age gaps may have an imbalance of power, which may result in the younger partner being coaxed into sex and failing to use protection.

So what do you do if your teen is under fourteen or is involved with an older partner? That depends on your teen, your relationship, and the situation at hand. Younger adolescents typically benefit from being involved in organized activities that broaden their range of friends and activities. Such involvement can help a teen give up sexual activity that feels premature. In addition, parental supervision at this age is critical. You might also consider seeking out the guidance of a qualified family therapist or psychologist.

For teens involved with an older partner, unless there's a clear-cut safety issue, we recommend against trying to banish a particular partner from your teen's life. Such a response will often result in a power struggle and can actually result in your teen clinging even more tightly to her partner than might otherwise be the case.

Still, you can set reasonable restrictions that limit the amount of time a teen spends without supervision and, at the very least, establish ground rules for behavior in the home. When you talk about the rules, don't make the partner a central issue. Some suggestions on how to do that:

- Instead of saying, "I don't want you staying out late with Brian," you might establish a curfew that limits the amount of time she can spend with him.
- Instead of saying, "You need to spend less time with Clara," you might try, "Saturday nights are yours for socializing, but Friday nights are family nights," and then plan a fun family activity each week.
- Instead of saying, "Jeff's not welcome in our home," you might explain why you feel a relationship with someone older worries you (and remind your teen about safer sex and birth control) and then set limits on when the partner can be in the home and behaviors that are acceptable to you. You might try, "I'm not comfortable with you having a boyfriend here while I'm not home. If I'm here, you can invite Jeff over, but bedrooms are off-limits for anyone of the opposite sex."

As difficult as it may be for you to do, you should seek to know as much as you can about your teen's partner. Getting to know the partner might feel counterintuitive (if you object to the person as a partner for your teen, should you really be so chummy?), but it serves several purposes. First, you may find your teen's partner isn't as objectionable as you first thought. Second, being able to observe your teen and her partner together gives you a chance to watch for red flags, such as signs of abusive or manipulative behavior. Third, refusing to have any contact with the partner, or forbidding contact between your teen and a particular partner, will likely damage your relationship and make it less likely for your teen to reach out to you should she experience any of those dangers you're so worried about. Finally, if you do see warning signs of abusive behavior or risky sexual activity, you'll have a better chance of getting your teen to talk or to acknowledge the problem (and do something about it).

At the same time, you should focus on talking to your teen about your values, expressing your concerns (in a nonjudgmental way) and encouraging her to come to her own conclusions about the relationship. If your teen is younger than fourteen, talk about why sexual relationships can be dangerous at this age (focus on the emotional risks outlined in chapter 6, and the risks for STIs and pregnancy in chapter 4). If your teen is involved in a relationship with someone more than four years older (or three years older for a teen under sixteen), talk about the research on STIs and pregnancy in such relationships and explain how a power imbalance can be harmful for the younger person.

Remember, too, that even after you've pointed out your concerns, your teen may not conclude that the relationship is problematic. Therefore, it makes sense to redouble your efforts to make sure your teen is practicing safer sex and using birth control.

One Way to Say It ...

Sixteen-year-old Carly is dating nineteen-year-old Jack, whom she met at a friend's party. Carly's mom has talked to her in the past about delaying sex until she feels she is ready emotionally, and also about safer sex and birth control. When they last spoke about it, Carly told her mom she was still a virgin. In recent days, Carly has talked about Jack and indicated the two are dating. Mom has just learned Jack's age and is concerned. She decides to talk to Carly about it, so she waits until Carly mentions her weekend plans with Jack and then brings up the subject in a light and friendly voice.

Mom:

It seems like you're really excited about Jack.

Carly:

I am. He's so amazing. All the girls think he's hot. I mean, he's like super-smart and funny and so cute.

Mom:

That's great, Carly. I'm happy for you. But I am worried about how much older Jack is. I've read a lot about teen relationships, and there have been studies that show that young girls like you who date older guys are much more likely to get pregnant or get an STI.

Carly:

Mom, please. Jack isn't like that. He's really responsible. And anyhow, we're not even having sex.

Mom:

That's good. I know last time we talked you felt like you weren't ready yet, and I agree with that. It's a big step. It's just that with an older partner, it's common for a younger girl to feel pressured to have sex, even if the partner's not intentionally pressuring her. You might feel like having sex would make you more grown-up, or that an older guy won't want to date someone who is still a virgin.

Carly:

Well, I guess I have thought about that. I mean, he is only human, you know? But he doesn't pressure me or anything.

Mom:

That's good. Have you two talked about having sex?

Carly:

A little. I told him I'm waiting. And anyhow, I would want to have birth control first, like we talked about. So I guess I would need to see a doctor first, like you said before.

Mom:

Yeah, that's the plan. And, you know, it would be important for you two to talk about what your expectations are for the relationship and for you to think about whether he's a person you can trust taking that step with. Sex can make the emotions so much more intense, and I don't want you to get hurt.

Carly:

I know, Mom. I don't want that either.

Mom:

Okay, and then you would also want to talk about if he's ever been tested for STIs or if he has any risk factors. We talked about that before, remember? It's things like injecting drugs and having any kind of sexual intercourse—including anal sex or oral sex— without a condom. I know it can be weird to talk about, but it's really important, Carly. If you want, I can give you information to give him about where to get tested.

Carly:

Okay. I'll be safe. And I'll get that number from you if we need it.

Teen Targeted: Wielding Influence

Under 15: Younger teens are more dependent on you, financially and emotionally, than they will be as they mature. That means you have leverage in establishing and enforcing rules and in giving privileges. Steps you can take:

- Limit unsupervised time and increase time in organized activities and with different social groups.
- Work on improving your teen's critical thinking and problem-solving skills by role-playing and considering various scenarios and potential outcomes.
- Help your teen understand and seek out healthy relationships.
- Talk to your teen about the imbalance of power that is common in relationships with a much older partner and the fact that young teens with older partners are more likely to have STIs or get pregnant.
- Make sure your teen has a realistic perception of norms for this age group. For teens dating someone older, it may seem like "everyone's having sex" (and, depending on the partner's age, everyone may well be), but within this age group the percentage of sexually active teens may actually be far lower.

15 to 17: As your teen gets older and less dependent, your ability to "stop" certain behaviors diminishes and the likelihood that you'll lose in a power struggle increases. Depending on the situation and your teen's age, you'll want to follow many of the above steps. But since sexual activity becomes more likely the older your teen gets, you'll want to focus especially on making sure your teen has the tools needed to stay safe sexually.

18 and over: Your ability to influence your teen's behavior is limited, but you're still a vital support person. Make an effort to be available for discussion, advice, or emotional support, and be on the lookout for warning signs of trouble. Be prepared to discuss them with your teen, and offer your support.

RISKY BUSINESS

How you feel about casual sex depends on your values. But it might also depend on who it is having sex. Parents, for example, may approach their sons' sexual encounters, even if they're not in the context of a relationship, with more of a wink and a nod than a gasp. A father (or mother, for that matter) might view any sexual activity as a boost to a boy's self-esteem, or an important part of male adolescence that paves the way for him to commit to one woman later.

Overall, though, most parents—and even most teens—would agree that casual sex or having multiple sexual partners presents a health risk, and in some cases an emotional risk, to boot. After all, having casual sex or more than four partners puts you at greater risk for STIs (remember that even condoms do not protect against all STIs, so sex always carries some degree of risk). And teens, especially girls, who take part in experimental or high-risk sexual activity are at higher risk for future depression than other teens (for boys, only high-risk sexual activity was linked to future depression).[71]

Still, there are teens (and adults) who prefer casual sexual encounters, engaging in anonymous or nearly anonymous sex, or having sex with numerous partners, for a variety of reasons. They may feel so inhibited that they can only have sex with a stranger, they may enjoy the thrill of a sexual conquest with no strings attached, they might be ashamed of their sexual orientation, or they may seek out anonymous partners for a host of other reasons.

If your teen is engaging in casual sex or sex with multiple partners, the discussions about sexual safety (chapter 5) and about household rules (chapter 7) become all the more important. It also may be helpful to think about and address the root cause. In some teens, inappropriate or destructive behavior—including high-risk sexual activity—can be a sign of low self-esteem or conflict within the family. They may be acting out in an attempt to get their parents' attention or assert their own authority. If that's the case, a mental health professional can help you make changes to make sure your teen's emotional needs are addressed.

Some teens also are unable to control their impulses, which could be a sign of immaturity or something else. Teens with attention deficit hyperactivity disorder (ADHD) may be particularly in need of help with controlling impulses. Hyper-manic sexual behaviors can also be a sign of early-onset bipolar disorder (recent research, on the other hand, has debunked the theory that teens self-medicate depression with sexual activity and drug use).

If you feel that your teen's behavior is driven by mental health or other issues beyond your control, it makes sense to seek out professional help. Your pediatrician, family medicine doctor, or local children's hospital can refer you to a psychologist who counsels teens. In addition, the American Psychological Association (www.apa.org) has an online database of psychologists, as does the Society for Adolescent Medicine (www.adolescenthealth.org).

If you suspect your teen is under the influence of alcohol or drugs, you have to recognize that part of the risk is lowered inhibitions, which may mean increased risk-taking in sexual activity. If you know that your teen is using alcohol or drugs, talk about your expectations and the consequences of breaking the rules. If the substance use seems like a more serious problem, you'll likely need to seek out professional help.

Sara's Story

Fifteen-year-old Sara was having trouble dealing with her parents' divorce. She was angry with both parents, but especially with her father, Bob, who, in a financial battle with her mother, had stopped paying Sara's private school tuition.

Sara, angry with her father and upset about the divorce, found comfort in her relationship with Dave, whom she had been seeing for three months. Sara's father, didn't like Dave, in part because Dave had dropped out of school and in part because he felt Sara was doing more of the relationship work than Dave did. Bob had noticed that Dave frequently borrowed money from Sara, canceled plans with her at the last minute so he could spend time with friends, and sometimes didn't call her back for days. Bob felt Sara deserved better, and he told her so.

One weekend when Sara was staying at her father's house, Bob arrived home early to find Sara and Dave naked in the master bedroom. Bob was angry that Sara was having sex, but even more upset by the fact that she'd had sex in her father's home and even in his bed. Bob argued with his daughter and forbade her to date Dave. Sara ignored him and continued not only to see Dave, but to sneak him into her father's house so that they could have sex.

Bob never made the connection between Sara's actions and the divorce or his own decision to stop paying her tuition. The two didn't talk about how Sara was feeling or why she continued to see Dave despite his lack of respect toward her.

Eventually Sara's mother, Diane, stepped in to mediate. She started with a simple observation: "It seems like you're really angry with Dad." From there, she gently suggested that Sara's anger might stem from her father's decision to stop paying her tuition. Sara at first insisted that her behavior with Dave had nothing to do with her father but eventually acknowledged that having sex in her father's bed—and even continuing to date Dave—might have been a way of striking back at him. Diane and Sara then talked about how Sara could express her anger with her father in a way that was responsible and healthy.

Over time, Sara also began to demand more respect from Dave, although the relationship eventually ended.

WHEN YOU FEAR ABUSE

Anyone, male or female, adult or teen, can fall victim to an abuser. But young women between the ages of sixteen and twenty-four may be most at risk. Of all the age groups, they experience the highest rates of intimate violence, with nearly 20 in 1,000 women reporting they are victims of abuse.[72]

That figure may actually underestimate the incidence of violence, since victims often are reluctant to report such crimes. In one national survey, one in five teens who had been in a serious relationship said they'd been hit, slapped, or pushed by a partner.[73] One in three said they'd been seriously concerned about being physically hurt by their partner. And 64 percent of teens said they'd had a partner who frequently acted jealous.

Beyond the immediate and future risk of physical harm at the hands of an abuser, abused girls face other risks: They are four to six times more likely to get pregnant and eight to nine times more likely to have tried to commit suicide.[74]

Sometimes it seems obvious that someone's in an abusive relationship. You may witness behavior you know to be abusive or see the unmistakable physical evidence of abuse. But more often, abuse is hidden, and victims themselves may not even identify the behavior as such. They may be convinced—often with the abuser's help—that they did something to deserve the treatment or that it's normal. They may have conflicting feelings for their abuser—hating the abuse, but feeling a strong attachment to the person. Most abusers have their good moments too, during which the relationship feels fun or comforting or exciting, making it even more confusing for the abused person.

You may need to identify for your teen exactly what constitutes an abusive relationship. Dating violence or abuse is a pattern of behaviors that one partner uses to control another. The abuse itself can be physical, sexual, or emotional, and an abuser can be male or female. An abusive partner might:

- try to control who his partner spends time with
- try to control how a partner spends her time or expresses herself, including by dictating how she dresses
- hit, punch, shake, squeeze, or physically harm a partner in some other way
- threaten a partner with physical harm
- continually pressure a partner for sex
- sexually assault a partner
- publicly or privately insult or humiliate a partner
- have explosive reactions or sudden mood swings
- blame the victim for the abusive behavior
- act unreasonably jealous or suspicious

Keep in mind that many abuse victims are reluctant to report abuse, and that teens may be particularly so because they fear their parents will be angry, overreact, or increase restrictions. Your teen most likely will not come to you to report abuse while still in a relationship with an abuser. There are some signs of abuse that you can watch for, however:

- unexplained bruises, broken bones, or other injuries
- withdrawal from friends and family
- sudden change in interest or participation in social activities
- sudden emotional outbursts
- absence from school and/or sudden drop in grades
- fear of upsetting a partner or changing her behavior out of fear or to avoid a fight

If you fear abuse, you should seek help. Two good resources are the National Teen Dating Abuse Helpline (www.loveisrespect.org) and the Dating Violence Resource Center on the National Center for Victims of Crime (www.ncvc.org) website (see our resource list at the back of this book for more detailed information).

And, of course, you should talk to your teen in a nonjudgmental way about the relationship, giving information about abusive relationships and, if possible, working with your teen to safely end the relationship.

One Way to Say It ...

Sixteen-year-old Deb has been dating John for three months. The two have an intense relationship with frequent, impassioned fights, mostly stemming from John's jealousy. Deb's mom overhears one argument in which it's clear John is being emotionally abusive. She talks to Deb the next morning ...

Mom:

Deb, I know that you really care about John, but I'm really worried about the way he treats you. I heard him yelling at you last night. He called you a slut, trash, a liar. That's abusive, Deb.

Deb:

> What? Mom, we were just fighting. He didn't mean it. He already texted me this morning and said he's sorry. He only yells like that because he loves me.

Mom:

> Honey, I don't think you're right about that. There's a website called Love Is Respect. Come to the computer. I want you to read this because I'm worried about you …

Even if your teen isn't currently in an abusive relationship, you should talk about abuse. It may help your teen spot the signs later or help a friend. When you do talk, remind your teen that:

- No one deserves to be threatened or harmed; violence is not a valid response to any behavior, period.
- Violent outbursts are often preceded by lesser abuses (such as a push, verbal abuse, or threatening comments), and violence in relationships can escalate suddenly. It's important to recognize the signs early and get out of the relationship before the behavior becomes extreme.
- You can't "change" an abuser. Staying in a relationship with the hope that you'll change someone is not only futile, but in the case of an abusive relationship, it's dangerous.
- You should report abuse. If a partner becomes violent, your teen should get to a safe place and then call the police.

If You Loved Me, You Would ...

When we love someone we do things to make them happy, right? And that's good, right? It's a reasonable question and one your teen might ask (and even if you're not the one she's asking, she may, at the very least, pose the question in her own mind).

If you've been talking about, or better yet, modeling loving behavior, you've likely addressed this in other forms. When we love someone, we sometimes do things that we don't particularly want to do—tagging along with him to get his car registered so he won't be bored, bringing him soup and Gatorade when he's sick, helping her study for a big exam. They're things we do for people we care about and part of being in a healthy relationship.

There are boundaries, of course, and they're not always clearly marked, so they bear discussion with your teen. Generally speaking, no one should do anything for someone else if it violates his personal values. Agreeing to have sex solely for the purpose of pleasing someone else (if it's not what you want to do) is a prime example.

Another vital element of healthy relationships is respect, and it applies to both parties. That means each person needs to respect the others' feelings and decisions. If a boy pressures his significant other to have sex or constantly complains, "You'd do it if you loved me" (we'll let him slide if he has the poor judgment to say it once), he's violating that rule. Ditto for a girl who does so to her partner. It's unhealthy and unfair, and it may qualify as abuse if it's persistent.

Such behavior is fairly common among teens. In one national study, 47 percent of teens said they'd done something that went against their beliefs for the sake of pleasing their partner (sixteen- to eighteen-year-olds were more likely to have done so than younger teens). One in four said they'd gone further than they wanted to sexually as a result of pressure from their partner.

So, what can your teen do when the "if you loved me" line rears its ugly head? First, treat it as just that, a line (and not a very original one). Second, a calm, firm "no" (repeating as often as necessary) is essential. Finally, your teen should follow up with, "If you loved me, you wouldn't pressure me." And be sure to send the message to your teen that doing so is a way of respecting yourself, which is the first step to gaining the respect of others.

Even if your teen doesn't take all threats seriously, you should. For teens under sixteen, and in cases where you fear for a teen's safety (no matter how old he or she is), that may mean alerting the authorities and taking steps to put distance between the teen and the abuser. In extreme cases, such as a partner who has a history of violence and incarceration, changing schools or moving away may be the only thing to do. And although we generally discourage parents from dictating who their teens date, if safety is a serious concern, that may be a step you need to take.

Remember, however, that disliking someone isn't a reason to banish her from your teen's life. You may hate her potty mouth or his motorcycle, but unless there's a safety issue, your most powerful tool will be shining a bright light on the behavior itself. Make yourself available to talk, and look for opportunities to discuss your teen's feelings and express your concerns.

If your teen's partner is sixteen or under, you might also alert the partner's parents, if you think it would be helpful (and keep in mind that it may not). If you do, be sure to use nonjudgmental words and tone. You might approach it as one parent asking another parent for help (for more on that, see chapter 9).

One Way to Say It ...

Sixteen-year-old Paige and seventeen-year-old Robby have been dating exclusively for six months. Paige's parents have known Robby for years as a nice, responsible teen. He has never shown any signs of violence, and Paige's parents feel fairly certain that he's not physically or sexually abusive. However, they worry about his demands that Paige spend all her time with him. When Paige mopes around after one argument, her father invites her for a walk and then brings up the subject ...

Dad:

Paige, you seem really upset. Do you want to talk about what's going on?

Paige:

No. Not really. It's just that Robby is being really mean and I can't stand it.

Dad:

What do you mean?

Paige:

Dad, you won't understand. You hate him anyway.

Dad:

I don't hate Robby, Paige. I do worry that he doesn't respect your feelings. It seems like he upsets you a lot.

Paige:

He's just acting really stupid. I have that track meet this weekend and he wants me to go to his basketball game. I can't do both.

Dad:

So you had to choose. That must have been hard.

Paige:

He says if I loved him I'd be there to cheer him on.

Dad:

It sounds like he is confused about love. He thinks being a couple means being joined at the hip—where he goes, you go. But this isn't really healthy in the long run. True love gives the person you love the space to do the things that make that person happy, even if it means doing them separately. It's a matter of respect. Like when Mom wanted to go back to school. I wanted her to be happy, but I also wanted her to be home at night with me and you. I gave her my blessing, even though we missed her, because I respect her right to fulfill her dreams.

Paige:

Yeah, I remember that time. We had fun watching *Danger Mouse* together, but I really missed Mom at bedtime.

Dad:

Look, maybe we can go over a way that you might talk to Robby about respect and your right to do the things that are important to you. Want to try that?

Paige:

Okay, I guess I'll try.

SEXUAL ASSAULT: WHEN SEX IS NOT CONSENSUAL

Most sex *is* consensual. But sexual assault does happen. In fact, women in their teens are by far the most at-risk age group for sexual assault, according to the U.S. Justice Department. Unfortunately, teens, and even adults, are often unclear on what exactly constitutes sexual assault.

The legal definition of sexual assault varies by state, so we can't tell you whether a certain scenario qualifies as sexual assault. In general, though, sexual assault refers to any unwanted physical contact of a sexual nature. Rape (also called forcible sexual assault) is typically defined as any penetration—genital, oral, or anal—by a part of the assailant's body or by an object, without the victim's consent.

Force doesn't have to be physical—a verbal threat or an implied threat can be enough—and a victim doesn't have to physically resist. Taking advantage of someone who cannot consent because they're incapacitated due to alcohol or drugs may also be considered sexual assault, since the victim was not able to consent to sex.

There are subcategories, too:

- Acquaintance rape (also called date rape) happens when the assailant is known to the victim.
- Statutory rape occurs when someone has consensual sexual contact with someone who is under the age of consent, which varies by state but usually falls between fourteen and eighteen (most states use sixteen as the age of consent). Some states do not consider it rape if the sexual contact is consensual and the partners are close in age (how close depends on the state). If the sexual partner is older and in a position of authority—a teacher, coach, or tutor, for example—stronger penalties may apply.

Keep in mind that victims of any type of sexual assault can be male or female and that sexual assaults are most often committed by someone the victim knows.

And know, too, that sexual assault is thought to be a grossly underreported crime. Acquaintance rape victims, in particular, often fail to label what happened to them as a crime. They may blame themselves for having been drunk, for having been alone with the assailant, or for what they wore, said, or did. They may feel ashamed, embarrassed, scared of retribution, or of what their parents or friends will think.

If you suspect or know that your teen is the victim of sexual assault, the first step is to label what happened as rape or sexual assault, or at least as potentially being rape or sexual assault. Your teen may be confused or conflicted and may not have identified it as such.

Then, even if it's not clear what happened but you fear a sexual assault of any type, you should take your teen to see a doctor, who can provide more education and take the appropriate medical steps. If the incident was recent, say the night before, it's best to go to the emergency room, preferably at a children's hospital if there is one nearby. Such hospitals typically see teens up to the age of eighteen (although at some the age is twenty-one) and have instruments that are appropriately sized for adolescents. They may also be more sensitive to your teen's emotional state. If there is no children's hospital nearby, you can go to the nearest emergency room, where they will have a protocol for treating victims of sexual assault.

Don't be surprised if your teen is reluctant to divulge details such as the assailant's name. Because sexual assaults are more likely to be committed by someone the victim knows, there can be a sense of betrayal and confusion. Your teen may not want to implicate the assailant. Or she may fear your reaction and worry about being punished or that you'll take matters into your own hands and confront the assailant.

As much as you want to see justice done, it's not helpful to try to force your teen to name names. Instead, focus on getting appropriate medical care. You might say, "Let's not even worry about that now. Let's just get you to a doctor."

At the hospital you'll likely be given contact information for a local rape crisis center, but if not, or if you're unsure about whether to go to the hospital, you can get help by calling the Rape, Abuse & Incest National Network (RAINN) Hotline at 800.656.HOPE (or get information online at www.rainn.org). RAINN can put you in touch with a local rape crisis center, which can, in many cases, arrange for a rape counselor to meet you at your local hospital.

RAINN also has an online crisis center with security measures in place to ensure victims' confidentiality. Your teen may find it more comfortable to seek help this way. Consider this example from RAINN's pilot test of the online crisis center: One teen who'd been sexually assaulted wasn't able to tell her mother. Instead, midway through an online counseling session, she brought her mother into her bedroom and showed her the computer screen. She couldn't speak the words, so she let the computer screen do it for her.

What to Do If You Know or Suspect Your Teen Has Been Sexually Assaulted

Take accusations seriously. Although false accusations do happen, they're fairly rare. Especially in the case of sexual abuse, it's important for victims to know that if they tell an adult, they'll be believed.

Seek help. The RAINN hotline can help you determine where to go and put you in touch with a local rape crisis center. If the crime wasn't recent, the hotline can offer suggestions on medical and mental health professionals who might be of help.

Retain evidence. In the case of a recent sexual assault, it's important to preserve the evidence of a crime, which means victims shouldn't bathe, douche, brush their teeth, or wash their clothes or hands, if possible (the fingernails may provide evidence that could help in a criminal prosecution).

Don't assign blame. Sexual assault is never a valid punishment for behavior of any kind. It's a message your teen needs to hear. That means that not only should you not accuse your teen of "asking for it"—an admonition that seems obvious to most parents—but also that you should be aware of making such an implication in your response to your teen. Asking, "Why did you go back to his room?" or "What were you thinking, getting drunk at that party?" and other loaded questions can send the message that the victim was somehow complicit in the crime.

Let your teen lead. Your teen may want to talk, or not. Sex crimes are disempowering, so whenever possible, allow your teen to decide how to respond. You can help by being supportive, understanding, and empathetic. If your teen doesn't want to talk, be sure to send the message that you're available if and when she is ready.

Watch for warning signs. People deal with trauma in different ways and in different time frames. Be on the watch for depression, anxiety, substance abuse, eating disorders, or other mental health issues (even long after the fact), and then steer your teen to the appropriate professional for help.

The Date Rape Drug

Date rape drugs have gotten a lot of attention in the media and on college campuses in particular in recent years. They are a potential nightmare: A drug that is undetectable by taste, sight, or smell when mixed into a drink and can incapacitate someone and leave her with no memory of being sexually assaulted.

There are at least three known date rape drugs, according to the U.S. Department of Health and Human Services. They are:

- GHB (gamma hydroxybutyric acid)
- Rohypnol (flunitrazepam)
- Ketamine (ketamine hydrochloride)

Although they're most often used by men to help in sexually assaulting women, victims can also be male.

Talk to your teen about how to reduce the risk of drug-assisted sexual assault. Here are some tips from the U.S. Department of Health and Human Services:

- Don't accept drinks from other people.
- Open containers yourself.
- Keep your drink with you at all times, even when you go to the bathroom.
- Don't share drinks.
- Don't drink from punch bowls or other large, common, open containers.
- Don't drink anything that tastes or smells strange (sometimes GHB tastes salty, for example).
- Have a nondrinking friend with you if you are drinking.
- If you suspect someone else has been given a date rape drug, call for help immediately.

If you think your teen has been drugged and sexually assaulted, it's important to seek help immediately, either by calling the police or by going to the hospital (you can also call a rape crisis hotline for help on what to do next). A urine test can detect the drugs, but they leave the body quickly (between twelve and seventy-two hours), so seeking help as soon as possible is important. It's also important to preserve any evidence, which means avoiding a bath, shower, or change of clothes before getting help.

GLBTQ Teens and Risky Behavior

Gay, lesbian, bisexual, transgender, and questioning (GLBTQ) teens are at risk for the same dangers as their straight counterparts, but they may also face additional challenges that straight teens don't. First, it's important to note that the stigma associated with certain sexual orientations and gender identities may make it harder for GLBTQ teens to seek help for problems. That's especially true if they haven't yet come out to friends and family or don't have support at home. A gay teen whose family thinks he's straight, for example, isn't likely to talk to his parents about whether his overly jealous boyfriend is being abusive or that he was sexually assaulted.

Gay teens may also be more likely to engage in high-risk behaviors such as sex with multiple or anonymous partners, in part because casual sexual encounters are accepted in some circles of gay culture and also because anyone who feels compelled to hide their orientation will likely have a harder time maintaining long-term relationships. (Although keep in mind that this is by no means a given—many gay teens don't engage in high-risk behaviors.)

Finally, GLBTQ teens may face harassment that their straight friends don't. In fact, GLBTQ teens report that violence, bullying, and harassment is fairly common. Four out of five GLBT students say they regularly hear homophobic remarks at school[75] (questioning students weren't identified as such in this study, so we've left off the Q). Nearly 40 percent report being verbally or physically assaulted, often with a weapon (transgender students report even more violence). Nearly one in three GLBT students skip school because they're afraid for their safety.

There are some warning signs to watch for if you're concerned your teen is facing harassment at school:

- fear of attending school
- skipping school or frequent unexplained illnesses that keep your teen home from school
- sudden change in interest or participation in extracurricular activities, or with certain social groups

If you're concerned, talk to your teen about any fears he may have and work to address those concerns.

If your teen is GLBTQ, you should also find out what the school's harassment policy is. Studies have found that teens in schools with a harassment policy that addresses orientation and gender identity are less likely to report violence and less likely to report having skipped school due to harassment or violence.

If there is no policy, work with your teen's school to develop one. The Gay, Lesbian, and Straight Education Network (GLSEN) offers resources for creating safe spaces and other information about GLBTQ teens and harassment (www.glsen.org/cgi-bin/iowa/all/home/index.html). The Gay-Straight Alliance for Safe Schools also has information and resources (www.gsaforsafeschools.org/about.html).

My Teen Is GLBTQ: Keith's Story

Keith had trouble in high school. He often fought with his father, who was a socially conservative political appointee. Keith rarely followed the rules at home or at school and was diagnosed with bipolar disorder. He was seeing a psychiatrist and was on medication to stop his outbursts of anger and manic acting out.

Keith also knew that he was gay and that his father would disapprove of his sexual orientation. Afraid to come out, Keith began to meet adult men online to have anonymous, unprotected sex. When he told his psychiatrist about these sexual encounters, his psychiatrist recommended he get tested for HIV. The test came back positive.

Keith was referred to a specialty clinic for teens with HIV. There he received psychological testing and learned that he had an IQ in the "very superior" range. All these years in school he had been bored.

Keith's father was enraged to find out that his son was gay and had been engaging in high-risk behavior. Keith's case manager suggested to Keith's father that Keith would be less likely to take health risks if he had an environment of acceptance at home. If he could date openly, he wouldn't be as likely to turn to anonymous encounters. The suggestion made Keith's father angry at first, but with the support of the treatment team, Keith's parents began to accept who he was. Keith enrolled in junior college, where he met a young man who was stable and compassionate (and whom Keith's parents liked).

They decided to move in together. The partner knew Keith's HIV status but was willing to be with him and hoped that the two of them could commit to a long-term, monogamous relationship. Keith's parents supported this.

Keith became more stable emotionally, took his medication as prescribed, and stopped engaging in risky behaviors. He is hoping to live into his fifties and that, by then, a cure will be found for AIDS. Keith's father has become much more sophisticated about the complexity of relationships and is now a member of PFLAG, a support group for parents of GLBTQ people. Ironically, becoming HIV positive turned Keith's life around for the better.

Depression: When to Worry

It's not uncommon for teens to feel sad or upset when a relationship ends, or if they're in a relationship that's stressful or unhealthy. But in some cases, feelings of sadness can veer off into the territory of clinical depression. Generally, signs of depression that persist for more than two weeks are cause to get professional help for your teen. The one exception is if your teen expresses suicidal thoughts or intentions. In that case, you should get help immediately.

Depression warning signs include:

- withdrawing from friends
- drastic changes in eating patterns
- an inability to sleep, or sleeping too much
- persistent feelings of sadness or hopelessness, or frequent crying spells
- a significant change in behavior or performance at school
- inability to concentrate, restlessness, or agitation
- loss of interest in hobbies or pursuits
- feelings of worthlessness
- giving prized possessions away (seek help immediately)
- suicidal expressions or thoughts or actions (seek help immediately)

Teens might also pretend to be sick, refuse to go to school, or suddenly act out at school. If you're concerned, seek help from a medical professional. A good place to start is with your teen's pediatrician or primary care physician, who can help determine whether further care is needed. You might also want to alert your teen's school counselor or teachers if you suspect a problem.

Hoping for the Best, Prepared for the Worst

If you're feeling a bit deflated after reading this chapter, we don't blame you. Thinking about the worst-case scenario can be upsetting.

But being informed is your best weapon—and one you can pass along to your teen. Even if your lives are gloriously free of red flags (which they probably will be), knowing what to watch for can help you spot problems early on and respond immediately and effectively.

CHAPTER 9

Talking about It:
When to Involve a Partner's Parents— and Your Family

As tempting as it may be, it's probably not going to be helpful to pull your daughter's boyfriend aside and bully him into doing a disappearing act. You might prevail, but it's far more likely that you'll do nothing more than drive a wedge between you and your daughter, and possibly even prod her to stay with him longer just to assert her independence. The same goes for your son and his love interest.

In fact, there are few circumstances under which you'd directly approach your teen's partner and expect to have a positive result. And while there aren't many more situations in which you'd find success talking to the parents of your teen's partner, there are a few cases where a conversation may be in order. They are:

- if your teen is under fourteen
- if your teen's partner is under fourteen
- if your teen's partner is under sixteen and you feel the partner may be at risk of pregnancy or an STI (for example, if you know your teen has an STI and you know the two had unprotected sexual contact)
- if the behavior occurred in the context of other risky behavior—say, under the influence of drugs or alcohol—and you feel the teen is at risk
- if you ask your teen and he says that having you talk to his partner's parents would be helpful

Even then, you'll also need to consider a few other factors.

Ask yourself:

- What am I hoping to accomplish by telling the other teen's parents? Be honest. If you're secretly hoping to build a parent-to-parent alliance with the aim of keeping two teens apart, you need to admit that to yourself. A valid motivation would be to make sure both teens are safe.
- Is there risky behavior involved? If you feel either teen is at risk and that reducing the risk can only be accomplished by talking to the teen's parents, then you should consider doing so.
- Can I accomplish the same ends by talking to my teen, rather than the other teen's parents?
- Is it possible that my actions will make things worse instead of better? Unless there are serious safety concerns, the older your teen is, the more likely you are to do harm to your relationship by taking the parent-to-parent route.
- Is my action likely to result in the teen being physically harmed by his parents? Keep in mind that even if the family seems "nice," you probably don't have a true understanding of the family dynamics involved. Some parents will not handle the news well and may even become violent toward their teenager. Most states allow teens over fourteen to access sexual health medical care and birth control, in part because of this reality.

Teen Targeted: Alerting the Other Parents

Under 15: If your teen is under fourteen, a talk with the partner's parents is likely in order, since a teen that young isn't mature enough to be sexually active. For a fourteen-year-old, you'll need to use your own judgment to determine whether the risk associated with contacting the other party is offset by the safety risk associated with the sexual behavior. If you do call, tell your teen you're doing so and ask for any information she has about the other teen's family life.

15 to 17: For fifteen- and sixteen-year-olds, you'll need to carefully weigh the potential downside of talking to a partner's parents—the risk for the partner and the risk of alienating your own teen—with any safety concerns you have. For seventeen-year-olds, you should only consider such contact if there are very serious safety concerns and the involvement of the teen's parents is somehow critical.

18 and over: We recommend against contacting the partner's parents, since any contact on your part will almost certainly fail to produce the desired result and will likely be seen by your teen as extremely intrusive (we see it that way, too, by the way).

Tread Lightly

If you decide to talk to the other parents, don't be surprised if they point the finger squarely at you (or your teen), especially if your revelation comes as a surprise to them.

You can minimize the chances of a defensive response by taking some suggestions:

- **Keep a neutral tone.** If you sound angry, your teen will be more defensive.
- **Don't call names or make judgments.** You can even say, "I'm not making any judgment calls," or something similar to signal to them that your motivation in calling is not one of placing blame.

- **State your purpose.** And no, "To tell you to keep your son away from my daughter," isn't an option. If they think you're trying to tell them how to parent, they'll probably become angry or shut you out. Instead, try, "I just wanted you to know that this happened," or "I wanted you to know so that you can make sure Jimmy gets tested."
- **State whatever action you've taken.** It might be, "I've already talked to my son about safer sex and the rules of our home," or "I took my daughter to see a doctor to talk about sexually transmitted infections and birth control."

One Way to Say It ...

Mom (on the phone with the mother of her daughter's boyfriend):

Hi, Laura, this is Cassie's mom, Michelle.

Laura:

Hi, Michelle, how are you?

Mom:

I'm fine, thanks. I'm calling because I was hoping to talk to you about Cassie and Jimmy. I'm not sure if you know they're dating.

Laura:

No, I didn't know.

Mom:

Well, I think they've been mostly seeing each other at friends' houses after school. I'm worried because Cassie is only fourteen, and she told me she and Jimmy have been having sex. And apparently they weren't using any protection. She was worried she was pregnant, although we did a pregnancy test and it was negative.

Laura:

Thank God for that. Well, I'm not very happy about it, but I'm not sure what you want me to do about it. You know how kids are.

Mom:

I just wanted you to be aware of the situation. I don't think they've been given a lot of information on condoms and birth control in school, but now that they're both sexually active they probably need it. I've talked to Cassie before about waiting to have sex, but I'm going to talk to her some more. And I'm going to take her to the gynecologist to get checked out. Do you want me to let you know if she is diagnosed with anything?

Laura:

Look, I appreciate your calling me, but I resent you acting like Jimmy has diseases or something. He's not like that.

Mom:

I didn't mean to imply that he had a disease. It's just that it's always a risk when people have unprotected sex. Thanks again for your understanding. Also, just to let you know, I told Cassie I would be talking to you today. So she may tell Jimmy.

Laura:

Okay, thanks. Goodbye.

It's probably not appropriate to involve your teen in this conversation or to force a sit-down between you and your teen and her partner. It's highly unlikely they'll feel comfortable talking about sex as a couple with you or in front of you (although if they're game, you're welcome to give it a go).

Approaching the Other Parents of a GLBTQ Couple

If your teen is gay, lesbian, bisexual, transgender, or questioning (GLBTQ), you'll likely have many of the same concerns you would with a straight teen. But because of the stigma still associated with being GLBTQ, you'll need to tread lightly when talking to a partner's parents. Some parents have a strongly negative reaction when first learning that their teen is gay, lesbian, bisexual, or transgender. They may even become violent or harshly punitive, which means that talking to a GLBTQ teen's parents may have serious consequences for the teen.

In fact, because orientation and gender identity can be such an emotionally charged issue, we recommend against talking to the partner's parents in almost every case. If you have a serious safety concern—you know that your teen has an STI and had unprotected sex with a partner, for example—we recommend talking to your teen's partner directly. In that case, use the same guidelines for minimizing a defensive response: keep a neutral tone, avoid judgmental statements, and state your purpose. One difference we'd recommend, though, is offering yourself as a resource, especially if the teen doesn't have a supportive environment at home. Answer questions yourself or direct your teen's partner to the appropriate health and support services.

Inside the Family: When to Talk and What to Say

Even when teens think they're being discreet (and there's no guarantee they'll really make the effort), chances are that members of the immediate family will eventually pick up on certain aspects of their private life.

That's especially true if your family dynamic is one in which everyone knows everything. In that case, you have a challenge — and a blessing. We'll tackle the challenge first: Since you've been used to discussing everything openly within your home, you may need to adjust to a new set of rules to respect your teen's right to privacy.

If your teen has confided in you, keep that confidence (unless there is a serious safety concern that can only be addressed by telling someone). Betraying that trust will almost certainly crush your teen's interest in talking openly in the future.

And remember the blessing: Older teens can act as a role model for younger siblings. If your teen is engaging in a healthy, loving relationship, that's something younger teens will pick up on. Ditto for modeling healthy habits in sexual decision making.

Studies have shown that older siblings can have a powerful influence on younger siblings' attitudes and sexual risk-taking behaviors.[76] Sibling relationships, after all, are some of the longest-lasting in a teen's life. And since siblings are closer than parents in age and status within the family, they fill a unique role that's part peer and part family, sharing perspectives and experiences in a way other family members and friends do not.

Younger siblings, then, often feel more comfortable getting advice and support from an older sibling than from a parent or even a friend.

And younger siblings may use their older sibling's sexual behaviors as a reference point in shaping their own behaviors and attitudes. One study, for example, found that younger teens whose older siblings believe that sex before age seventeen is inappropriate are more likely to delay having sex for the first time.[77]

It's also important to note that older siblings often feel protective of younger siblings and may therefore try to steer them clear of harm by talking about condoms or birth control, for example. This is true even when older siblings are engaging in sexual risk-taking themselves. Of course, influence varies depending on the strength of the bond between siblings. Studies have found that siblings who considered themselves close to older siblings were more likely to report turning to their sibling for advice and support.

Even if your teen doesn't want to make it family business— or does so without your knowledge or involvement—you can at the very least use your ongoing discussion about sex with your older teen as a reminder to open an age-appropriate conversation with younger siblings. If you haven't already, invest in a good, age-appropriate book that explains anatomy, reproduction, sex, and relationships (see resources for some suggestions).

And when you do talk to younger siblings, be sure to:

- **Talk about your values.** Open an age-appropriate conversation about how you feel about sex, when you think it's appropriate for teens, and why you feel that way.
- **Talk about responsibilities and privileges.** You might explain that in your house, sleeping in the same bed is reserved for adults only (or married couples, or whatever your rule is). Or that spending the night with another person (say, on vacation) is only okay for people who are over eighteen. Remember the authoritative parent. It's okay to set an age limit or other conditions for certain privileges.
- **Talk about safer sex.** Discuss condoms, birth control, and why sexual relationships require maturity.
- **Offer to answer questions they have about their older sibling.** They may be curious about their big brother's girlfriend or about love, sex, and growing up. Use that curiosity to educate them. But steer the conversation to the general to avoid revealing personal information.
- **Prepare to be fair and beware of the double standard.** If you allow your seventeen-year-old son to sleep at his girlfriend's house, your daughter should have the same treatment

at the same age, or you should have a good reason for not giving her the same independence ("because she's a girl" is *not* a good reason).

Rita's Story

Remember Rita and her daughter, Lynn, from chapter 3? After Lynn revealed to her mother that she had lost her virginity years before, the two sat down to talk about Lynn's relationship with her current boyfriend.

Lynn said that as a younger teen she felt Rita didn't want to discuss sex, and so Lynn avoided talking to her about it. Rita was surprised. She had always felt she had an open relationship with her daughter and had said more than once, "You can talk to me about anything." Lynn explained that other things Rita said had given her the message that her mother wouldn't be open-minded when talking about sex.

As the two were talking, Lynn's fifteen-year-old sister, Debbie, walked by the room. Hearing the two talk, she hovered for a moment and then asked if she could join the discussion. Rita left the decision up to Lynn, who said she was comfortable with her sister being present. Rita asked Debbie if she felt as Lynn did—that sex wasn't something they could talk about in their house. Debbie, although she was naturally inclined to avoid hurting her mother's feelings, admitted that she would be very nervous about broaching the subject with Rita.

Rita explained that she had grown up in a household where personal matters, like sex, were clearly not on the table for discussion. She acknowledged that although she'd tried hard to do the opposite as a parent, her own discomfort had probably shone through to her daughters.

Seizing on the opportunity, she told Debbie how she felt about teens and sex—that sex was something special that should be saved for a committed relationship and preferably not experienced until a teen is old enough to handle all the complexities. She then assured Debbie that she really was open to talking about anything Debbie wanted to talk about—even sex—and that she would work hard to do so without being judgmental. "I feel terrible that Lynn couldn't come to me when she probably really needed me. I want to make sure that doesn't happen again," she told Debbie.

She and Lynn then finished their conversation about Lynn's decision regarding sex with her current boyfriend. They talked about birth control and the risks of becoming even more emotionally attached. Rita pointed out to Lynn that having sex might make breaking up more difficult. The two talked about how serious Lynn and her boyfriend were and whether she saw them having a future together. Debbie listened quietly.

Later, when Rita was alone, Debbie approached her with a question she'd been tossing around in her mind. "Did you and Dad have sex before you were married?" she asked. The question gave Rita a chance to tell Debbie something she never had before—that she had waited until she was nineteen to have sex and then did so with a man she thought she was going to marry. The relationship fell apart, and Rita was devastated. The experience in part shaped her view that her daughters should wait as long as possible to have sex. Debbie and Rita were able to talk more about why that was, and as Debbie matured, they continued to talk about sex and relationships.

PSSST. DON'T TELL GRANDMA!

You may have a lot in common with the people in your family—from that button nose you all share to the memories of Grandma's homemade pasta—but in the end, all families are made up of individuals. That means in most families, there will be a range of values and a varying degree of acceptance of other peoples' values. Some greet other people's lifestyles and decisions with open arms; others do not.

When you're dealing with those who do not, it's tempting to avoid confrontation (or disapproval). But generally speaking, while it's fine to keep your private life private, it's usually not healthy to lie outright—going to great lengths to keep Grandma from finding out her granddaughter is spending every weekend at her boyfriend's house, for example. If you're stuffing a pillow under your daughter's blanket in hopes that Grandma will think she's merely sleeping late every Saturday morning, you're probably taking the lie a little too far.

Unless the person in question is emotionally disturbed or presents a serious risk to the teen (for example, a parent who might disown or evict a teen), it's usually best to be as honest as you can. You might actually be surprised by family members' ability to adapt.

If you're hiding reality from younger siblings, consider how you can be honest with them in a way that is age-appropriate and even productive. If your eighteen-year-old is sleeping at his girlfriend's house every weekend, for example, and your thirteen-year-old wants to know where he is, you *could* make up an elaborate lie. But a better approach would be to explain the situation. In doing so you would, of course, talk about your values and explain the rights and responsibilities that an eighteen-year-old has in your home. Will your younger teen decide at eighteen that she, too, will sleep at a partner's house? Maybe. But if you've had five years to talk to her about values, safety, and the emotional aspects of sexual relationships, you'll at least be assured she has the tools she needs to make an informed decision.

Ask the Expert …

Q: My seventeen-year-old daughter has been dating the same boy for a year. Recently, I was getting the car keys from her purse and found a package of birth control pills. When I asked her about it she said she wasn't having sex, but as we talked she admitted she was. We argued. Her father and I feel strongly that sex before marriage is wrong, so her behavior really made me upset. In the end, she stormed out and we didn't resolve anything. She is very committed to her boyfriend and continues to see him.

There is a lot of tension in our home over this issue. And I'm afraid that her fifteen-year-old sister is going to think it's okay to have sex whenever she wants because we're letting her older sister date this guy. I'm not sure what to do. Right now, my seventeen-year-old and I are barely speaking, and I haven't talked at all to her younger sister about what's going on.

A: There are two big, interrelated concerns here: how to move forward with your older daughter and what to tell your younger daughter.

Let's start with your seventeen-year-old. The first step is to reopen the conversation with her. Ask her if the two of you can sit down for a private conversation to talk about what's going on in her life. Then, clear some of the tension so you can have a helpful conversation. One way to do this is to acknowledge that you've been upset and that the revelation caught you by surprise. If you said things in anger that were hurtful or judgmental, apologize now. Once you've done that, you can explain why you were so upset—that your values are such that you think sex before marriage is wrong. Then, be honest about what that means for her. First, reassure her that you love her and respect her. If you're having a hard time accepting that her values aren't the same as yours, tell her that as well.

Since she is already sexually active, your chief concern here must be to make sure she's safe. And on that front, there's room for praise. She is using birth control, which shows responsibility (and that she has already seen a doctor). However, it's not clear whether or not she has been protected from STIs.

When you talk to her, you may want to gently prod for answers to a few questions:

- Has she talked to her boyfriend about his sexual history?
- Is he using condoms?
- Has he been tested for STIs?
- Has she been tested for STIs?
- Have they talked about what they would do if she became pregnant?

And, of course, send the message that if she's going to have sex, she needs to protect herself by limiting the number of sexual partners, avoiding high-risk behaviors, and always using birth control and a condom.

Your second concern, of course, is your younger daughter. It's unlikely that she'll think "it's okay to have sex whenever I want" because her sister is in a sexual relationship. But it is highly likely that she has questions about sex, about love, and about her sister's relationship with you and your husband, among other things. If you haven't already, find a teachable moment to open a conversation.

Just as you did for her older sister, you'll want to talk about your values and why you feel sex before marriage is wrong. Acknowledge the tension in the house (she already knows it's there) and explain that you're working on it with her sister. Remind her that you love them both. And while you shouldn't violate your older teen's privacy, you can offer to answer any general questions your younger daughter has.

In the ongoing conversation you have with her, be sure to talk about:

- birth control and STI protection
- the emotional aspects of sexual relationships
- her right to say no—at any time and with anyone
- the rights and responsibilities she has in your home (including the right to talk to you about sex and relationships)

Be sure to keep the conversation going over time. As she moves through the teen years, she'll likely have new concerns and questions that you can help answer.

GLBTQ Teens and the Family

Although we don't recommend going to great lengths to deceive anyone about a teen's sex life, the reality is that gay, lesbian, bisexual, transgender, and questioning (GLBTQ) teens still face discrimination, harassment, and violence, sometimes within their own families.

If you feel that your GLBTQ teen would be in physical danger or would be harshly punished by someone in the family because of his orientation or gender identity, you'll need to make the call about how far to go in hiding the truth.

If you're worried about how younger siblings will respond to an older sibling's orientation or gender identity, a good book can help present it in an age-appropriate way (see the back of this book for a list of resources). Be sure, of course, to heed the wishes of your GLBTQ teen. That means respecting the wishes of teens who aren't ready to come out to the entire family. But at the same time you should work to create an environment in which your teen will feel more comfortable doing so.

DOS AND DON'TS FOR CREATING AN ENVIRONMENT OF ACCEPTANCE IN YOUR FAMILY:

- Don't assume everyone is straight until proven otherwise.
- Do present the possibilities for love, marriage, and commitment in a gender-neutral way (for example, by saying, "When you grow up you'll meet someone you love and decide to be in a committed relationship" rather than, "When you grow up you'll meet a great guy and marry him").
- Don't tolerate homophobic statements. Speak up when you hear them and teach your teens about the harm they cause.
- Do find out what your kids are learning in school and then supplement it, if necessary, with information on what it means to be gay, lesbian, bisexual, transgender, or questioning. They may find the information applies to a sibling, themselves, a parent, or a friend. Or they might not. Either way, talking about it will help dispel myths and misunderstandings.

PFLAG and other groups also offer resources for helping family members come to terms with a loved one's orientation or gender identity. See the back of this book for more resources.

Acknowledgments

Many thanks to Kate Epstein at Epstein Literary and Jill Alexander at Fair Winds Press for helping deliver this book from concept to reality and to Laura B. Smith and Julia Maranan for their fine editing.

Thanks also go out to a host of colleagues and friends for their support, time, and expertise. They are: Irene Addlestone and Teens Against the Spread of AIDS (TASA) at Children's National Medical Center; Deborah Asher-Hertzber, L.C.S.W.; Michelle Barratt, M.D.; Donald Cavanaugh at Safe Schools South Florida; Lawrence J. D'Angelo, M.D., at Children's National Medical Center; Marla Eisenberg, Sc.D., M.P.H.; Michael Hertzberg, M.D.; Barbara Huberman at Advocates for Youth; Katherine Hull and Gretchen Anderton at RAINN; Guy van Syckle, Ph.D.; Adam Ratliff at PFLAG; Robert Weigl, Ph.D.; Catherine Winter, Ph.D.; and Fred Wyand at the American Social Health Association.

And most important, we'd like to thank our husbands, Spiro Antoniades and George Lyon, and our families for their support, wisdom, and encouragement.

About the Authors

Maureen E. Lyon, Ph.D., A.B.P.P., is a licensed clinical psychologist and associate research professor in pediatrics at the George Washington University Medical Center and in the Division of Adolescent and Young Adult Medicine at Children's National Medical Center in Washington, DC.

A former junior high school teacher and mother of two (now in their twenties), she earned a Ph.D. in clinical psychology from American University in 1991. She holds a diplomate in health psychology from the American Board of Professional Psychology and is a member of the Society for Adolescent Medicine.

All of Dr. Lyon's research interests and efforts focus on the study of adolescence. In 1990 she became the first psychologist to work with HIV-positive teens for the Burgess Clinic in the Department of Adolescent and Young Adult Medicine, where she still works and trains residents, medical students, and adolescent medicine fellows. She has extensive experience in dealing with teens and HIV/AIDS and in counseling families and teens. She currently has a general private practice with adults in Alexandria, Virginia, with a specialty in health psychology. She is coauthor of the book *Teenagers, HIV, and AIDS: Insights from Youths Living with the Virus*. For more information about Dr. Lyon, visit www.apapo.org/DrMaureenLyon.

Christina Breda Antoniades is a freelance journalist with seventeen years of experience writing for print and online publications, including the *Washington Post*, *Baltimore* magazine, Discovery Health Channel online, and www.revolutionhealth.com. She has written extensively about health and parenting topics and is also a mother of three. You can learn more about her at www.christinaantoniades.com.

Resources

FOR TEENS

Advocates for Youth, Youth Lounge: www.advocatesforyouth.org/youth/index.htm

Coalition for Positive Sexuality: www.positive.org/Home/index.html

Go Ask Alice (Columbia University): www.goaskalice.columbia.edu/index.html

I Wanna Know (American Social Health Association): www.iwannaknow.org

MTV's Think: http://think.mtv.com/Issues/relationshipsexuality

Scarleteen: www.scarleteen.com

Sex, etc: www.sexetc.org

SexTalk: www.sextalk.org

Stay Teen (National Campaign to Prevent Teen Pregnancy): www.stayteen.org

Teenwire (Planned Parenthood Federation of America): www.teenwire.com

FOR PARENTS

Advocates for Youth: www.advocatesforyouth.org

SIECUS (Sexuality Information and Education Council of the United States): www.siecus.org

Revolution Health National Campaign to Prevent Teen Pregnancy: www.teenpregnancy.org

Parenting Teens Online: www.parentingteensonline.com

FOR GLBTQ TEENS AND FAMILIES

Out Proud (The National Coalition for Gay, Lesbian, Bisexual & Transgender Youth): www.outproud.org

Parents, Families & Friends of Lesbians and Gays: http://pflag.org

Matthew's Place: www.matthewshepard.org

National Youth Advocacy Coalition: www.nyacyouth.org

The Trevor Project (a crisis and suicide prevention site, including helpline): www.thetrevorproject.org/home1.aspx

YouthResource (a project of Advocates for Youth): www.youthresource.com

ABOUT PREGNANCY AND STIS

Centers for Disease Control and Prevention (with information and resources on a host of STIs and HIV): www.cdc.gov/STD

HIVtest.org (information on HIV and STIs): 800.458.5231; www.hivtest.org

Not-2-Late (emergency contraception): www.Not-2-Late.com

Sex, etc.org (a website and magazine operated by teens, for teens): www.sexetc.org

The American Social Health Association: STI resource center hotline 919.361.8488; prerecorded STI information 800.227.8922; www.ashastd.org and www.iwannaknow.org

Planned Parenthood: Health center locator 800.230.7526; www.plannedparenthood.org or www.teenwire.com for teens

The Body (HIV/AIDS resource): www.thebody.com

The National Women's Health Information Center (run by the U.S. Department of Health and Human Services): www.4woman.gov (or for information on emergency contraception, go to www.4woman.gov/FAQ/birthcont.htm)

ON DATING VIOLENCE AND SEXUAL ASSAULT

Choose Respect: www.chooserespect.org/scripts/index.asp

Men Can Stop Rape: www.mencanstoprape.org

National Domestic Violence Hotline: www.ndvh.org

National Sexual Assault Hotline: 800.656.HOPE

Office On Violence Against Women:
www.enditnow.gov/sa/flash.html

RAINN (Rape, Abuse, & Incest National Network) national sexual
assault hotline: 800.656.4673; www.rainn.org

United States Department of Justice:
www.ovw.usdoj.gov/teen_dating_violence.htm

BOOKS FOR PARENTS

*Always My Child: A Parent's Guide to Understanding Your Gay,
Lesbian, Bisexual, Transgendered or Questioning Son or Daughter.* Kevin Jennings with Pat Shapiro. New York: Fireside, 2003.

*Crossing Paths: How Your Child's Adolescence Triggers Your Own
Crisis.* Laurence Steinberg with Wendy Steinberg. New York:
Simon & Schuster, 2000.

Parents and Adolescents Living Together. Gerald R. Patterson and
Marion S. Forgatch. Champaign, IL: Research Press, 2005.

*Why Do They Act That Way? A Survival Guide to the Adolescent
Brain for You and Your Teen.* David Walsh. New York: Free
Press, 2004.

BOOKS FOR TEENS

*S.E.X.: The All-You-Need-to-Know Progressive Sexuality Guide to
Get You through High School and College.* Heather Corinna.
New York: Da Capo Press, 2007.

GLBTQ: The Survival Guide for Queer and Questioning Teens. Kelly
Heugel. Minneapolis: Free Spirit Publishing, 2003.

The Guy Book: An Owner's Manual. Mavis Jukes. New York:
Random House, 2002.

*The Teenage Guy's Survival Guide: The Real Deal on Girls, Growing
Up, and Other Guy Stuff.* Jeremy Daldry. New York: Hachette
Book Group, 1999.

Hang-Ups, Hook-Ups, and Holding Out: Stuff You Need to Know
about Your Body, Sex, and Dating. (for girls) Melissa Holms and
Trish Hutchison. Deerfield Beach, FL: Health Communications
Inc., 2007.

BOOKS FOR YOUNG TEENS AND CHILDREN

It's Perfectly Normal. Changing Bodies, Growing Up, Sex and Sexual Health. Robie H. Harris, illustrated by Michael Emberley. Somerville, MA: Candlewick Press, 2004.

It's Not the Stork: A Book about Girls, Boys, Babies, Bodies, Families, and Friends. (for younger children) Robie H. Harris, illustrated by Michael Emberley. Somerville, MA: Candlewick Press, 2008.

It's So Amazing: A Book about Eggs, Sperm, Birth, Babies, and Families. (for younger children) Robie H. Harris, illustrated by Michael Emberley. Somerville, MA: Candlewick Press, 2004.

The What's Happening to My Body Book for Boys. (ages 8 to 15) Lynda Madaras and Area Madaras. New York: Newmarket Press, 2007.

The What's Happening to My Body Book for Girls. (ages 9 to 12) Lynda Madaras and Area Madaras. New York: Newmarket Press, 2007.

Notes

1   *Trends in the Prevalence of Sexual Behavior.* Youth Risk Behavior Surveillance (YRBS), Centers for Disease Control, 2007.

2   Kendall Powell, "Neurodevelopment: How Does the Teenage Brain Work?" *Nature* (August 24, 2006).

3   David Walsh, *Why Do They Act That Way? A Survival Guide to the Adolescent Brain for You and Your Teen* (New York: Free Press, 2004).

4   American Academy of Pediatrics, *Helping Your Child Cope with Life*, 2006.

5   Kaiser Family Foundation, "Generation M," March 2005, www.kff.org/entmedia/entmedia030905pkg.cfm.

6   Kaiser Family Foundation, "Sex on TV 4," November 2005, www.kff.org/entmedia/entmedia110905pkg.cfm.

7   The National Campaign to Prevent Teen Pregnancy, *With One Voice: America's Adults and Teens Sound Off about Teen Pregnancy,* 2007.

8   Jason S. Carroll, Laura Padilla-Walker, Larry J. Nelson, Chad D. Olson, Carolyn McNamara Barry, and Stephanie D. Madsen, "Generation XXX: Pornography Acceptance and Use Among Emerging Adults," *Journal of Adolescent Research* 23, no. 1 (2008): 6–30.

9   T. Tydén, S.E. Olsson, and E. Häggström-Nordin, "Improved Use of Contraceptives, Attitudes toward Pornography, and Sexual Harassment among Female University Students," *Women's Health Issues* (2001). Also, C. Rogala and T. Tydén, "Does Pornography Influence Young Women's Sexual Behaviour?" *Women's Health Issues* (2003).

10 Steven C. Martino, Rebecca L. Collins, Marc N. Elliott, Amy Strachman, David E. Kanouse, and Sandra H. Berry, "Exposure to Degrading Versus Non-Degrading Music Lyrics and Sexual Behavior among Youth," *Pediatrics* (August 2006).

11 Centers for Disease Control and Prevention, *Youth Risk Behavior Surveillance (YBRS)*, 2007.

[12] Centers for Disease Control and Prevention, *Youth Risk Behavior Surveillance (YBRS)*, 2007.

[13] University of Minnesota, "Reducing the Risk: Connections That Make a Difference in the Lives of Youth," http://allaboutkids. umn.edu/cfahad/Reducing_the_risk.pdf.

[14] National Center for Health Statistics, "Teenagers in the United States: Sexual Activity, Contraceptive Use, and Childbearing, 2002," *Vital and Health Statistics*, Series 23, no. 24 (2004).

[15] Ibid.

[16] The National Campaign to Prevent Teen Pregnancy, *With One Voice: America's Adults and Teens Sound Off about Teen Pregnancy*, 2007.

[17] Centers for Disease Control and Prevention, *Youth Risk Behavior Surveillance (YBRS)*, 2007.

[18] University of Minnesota, "Reducing the Risk: Connections that Make a Difference in the Lives of Youth," http://allaboutkids. umn.edu/cfahad/Reducing_the_risk.pdf.

[19] Ibid.

[20] National Campaign to Prevent Teen Pregnancy, *Families Matter: A Research Synthesis of Family Influences on Adolescent Pregnancy.* Washington, DC, 1998.

[21] T.E. Mueller, L.E. Gavin, and A. Kulkarni, "The Association between Sex Education and Youth's Engagement in Sexual Intercourse, Age at First Intercourse, and Birth Control Use at First Sex," *Journal of Adolescent Health* 42, no. 1 (2008).

[22] National Center for Health Statistics, *National Survey of Family Growth*, www.cdc.gov/nchs/NSFG.htm.

[23] Laura Duberstein Lindberg, Rachel Jones, and John S. Santelli, "Non-Coital Sexual Activities Among Adolescents," *Journal of Adolescent Medicine* (July 2008).

[24] Bonnie L. Halpern-Felsher, Jodi L. Cornell, Rhonda Y. Kropp, and Jeanne M. Tschann, "Oral Versus Vaginal Sex among Adolescents: Perceptions, Attitudes, and Behavior," *Pediatrics* (2005).

[25] Ibid.

26   Melina M. Bersamin, Deborah A. Fisher, Samantha Walker, Douglas L. Hill, and Joel W. Grube, "Defining Virginity and Abstinence: Adolescents' Interpretations of Sexual Behaviors," *Journal of Adolescent Health* (August 2007).

27   Laura Duberstein Lindberg, Rachel Jones, and John S. Santelli, "Non-Coital Sexual Activities Among Adolescents," *Journal of Adolescent Medicine* (July 2008).

28   Lawrence B. Finer, "Trends in Premarital Sex in the United States, 1954–2003," The Guttmacher Institute (January–February 2007).

29   The National Campaign to Prevent Teen Pregnancy, *With One Voice: America's Adults and Teens Sound Off about Teen Pregnancy*, 2007.

30   Kristen McGinty, David Knox, and Marty E. Zusman, "Friends with Benefits: Women Want 'Friends,' Men Want 'Benefits,' *College Student Journal* (December 2007).

31   Melissa A. Bisson and Timothy R. Levine, "Negotiating a Friends with Benefits Relationship," *Archives of Sexual Behavior* (September 13, 2007).

32   Willam D. Mosher, Anjani Chandra, and Jo Jones, "Sexual Behavior and Selected Health Measures: Men and Women 15 to 44 Years of Age, United States, 2002," Division of Vital Statistics, Centers for Disease Control and Prevention (September 15, 2005).

33   Centers for Disease Control and Prevention, *Youth Risk Behavior Surveillance (YBRS)*, 2007.

34   National Institute on Drug Abuse, "Monitoring the Future," www.monitoringthefuture.org.

35   The National Campaign to Prevent Teen Pregnancy, *With One Voice: America's Adults and Teens Sound Off about Teen Pregnancy*, 2007.

36   Ibid.

37   Ibid.

38   Ibid.

39   L.D. Lindberg, "Changes in Formal Sex Education: 1995–2002," *Perspectives on Sexual and Reproductive Health* (2006).

40 Laura Duberstein Lindberg, John S. Santelli, and Susheela Singh, "Changes in Formal Sex Education: 1995–2002." *Perspectives on Sexual and Reproductive Health* (December 2006).

41 Lawrence B. Finer, "Trends in Premarital Sex in the United States," *Public Health Reports* 23, no. 73 (2007).

42 C. Trenholm, et al, "Impacts of Four Title V, Section 510 Abstinence Education Programs Final Report," Princeton, NJ: Mathematic Policy Research, 2007.

43 Pamela Kohler, et al, "Abstinence-Only and Comprehensive Sex Education and the Initiation of Sexual Activity and Teen Pregnancy," *Journal of Adolescent Health* (March 2008).

44 Guttmacher Institute, "U.S. Teenage Pregnancy Statistics: National and State Trends and Trends by Race and Ethnicity," (September 2006).

45 National Center for Health Statistics, "Teenagers in the United States: Sexual Activity, Contraceptive Use, and Childbearing, 2002," *Vital and Health Statistics*, Series 23, no. 24 (2004).

46 National Health Information Network, "Teen Pregnancy Prevention," www.neahin.org/programs/reproductive/teenpreg.htm.

47 Lawrence B. Finer, et al, "Disparities in Rates of Unintended Pregnancy in the United States, 1994 and 2001," *Perspectives on Sexual and Reproductive Health* (2006).

48 Guttmacher Institute, "U.S. Teenage Pregnancy Statistics: National and State Trends and Trends by Race and Ethnicity," (September 2006).

49 National Center for Health Statistics, *National Vital Statistics Reports* 52, no. 10 (2003).

50 Guttmacher Institute, "U.S. Teenage Pregnancy Statistics: National and State Trends and Trends by Race and Ethnicity," (September 2006).

51 L.A. Dauphinee, Guttmacher Institute, March 2006.

52 Guttmacher Institute, "Parental Involvement in Minors' Abortions," *State Policies in Brief* (August 1, 2006).

53 H. Weinstock, et al, "Sexually Transmitted Diseases among American Youth: Incidence and Prevalence Estimates, 2000,"

Perspectives on Sexual and Reproductive Health 36, no. 1 (2004): 6–10.

[54] Centers for Disease Control and Prevention, *Youth Risk Behavior Surveillance (YBRS)*, 2005.

[55] Centers for Disease Control and Prevention, "HIV/AIDS," www.cdc.gov/hiv.

[56] Centers for Disease Control and Prevention, *Youth Risk Behavior Surveillance (YBRS)*, 2007.

[57] The National Campaign to Prevent Teen Pregnancy, *With One Voice: America's Adults and Teens Sound Off about Teen Pregnancy*, 2007.

[58] Colorado Coalition Against Sexual Assault, www.ccasa.org.

[59] Kenneth R. Ginsburg, 2007.

[60] The National Campaign to Prevent Teen Pregnancy, *With One Voice: America's Adults and Teens Sound Off about Teen Pregnancy*, 2007.

[61] Colorado Coalition Against Sexual Assault.

[62] Ibid.

[63] Suzanne Ryan, Kerry Franzetta, Jennifer Manlove, and Emily Holcombe, "Discussions about Contraception or STDs with Partners Prior to First Sex," *Perspectives on Sexual and Reproductive Health* (September 2007).

[64] Ibid.

[65] Marla Eisenberg, Diann Ackard, Dianne Neumark-Sztainer, and Michael Resnick, "Casual Sex and Emotional Health in Sexually Active Young Adults: Are Friends with Benefits Psychologically Damaging?" Presented at the annual meeting of the Society for Adolescent Medicine, Spring 2008.

[66] Li, Feigelman, and Stanton, 2000; Miller, Forehand, and Kotchick, 1999; Rai, Stanton, Wu, Li, and Galbraith, et al., 2003. "Biological, Familial, and Peer Influences on Dating in Early Adolescence," *Archives of Sexual Behavior* (December 2007),

[67] J. Dennis Fortenberry, Barry P. Katz, Margaret J. Blythe, Beth E. Juliar, Wanzhu Tu, and Donald P. Orr, "Factors Associated with Time of Day of Sexual Activity among Adolescent Women," *Journal of Adolescent Health* (March 2006).

68 David Knox, Kristen McGinty, Marty E. Zusman, and Jennifer Gescheidler, "Deception of Parents During Adolescence," *Adolescence* (Fall 2001).

69 Janis Wolak, David Finkelhor, Kimberley J. Mitchell, and Michelle L. Ybarra, "Online 'Predators' and Their Victims: Myths, Realities, and Implications for Prevention and Treatment," *American Psychologist* 63, no. 2 (February/March 2008).

70 S. Ryan, K. Franzetta, J.S. Manlove, et al, "Older Sexual Partners during Adolescence: Links to Reproductive Health Outcomes in Young Adulthood," *Perspectives on Sexual and Reproductive Health* (March 2008).

71 Denise D. Hallfors, Martha W. Waller, Daniel Bauer, Carol A. Ford, and Carolyn T. Halpern, "Which Comes First in Adolescence—Sex and Drugs or Depression?" *American Journal of Preventive Medicine* (October 2005).

72 U.S. Department of Justice, "Intimate Partner Violence," May 2000.

73 "Controlling Behavior in Teen Relationships," Liz Claiborne Inc., March 2006.

74 Jay G. Silverman, Anita Raj, and Karen Clements, "Dating Violence against Adolescent Girls and Associated Substance Use, Unhealthy Weight Control, Sexual Risk Behavior, Pregnancy, and Suicidality," *Pediatrics* (August 2004).

75 Gay, Lesbian, and Straight Education Network (GLSEN), *National School Climate Survey*, 2003.

76 Amanda K. Kowal and Lynn Blinn-Pike, "Sibling Influences on Adolescents' Attitudes toward Safe Sex Practices," *Family Relations* (July 2004).

77 E.D. Widmer, "Influence of Older Siblings on Initiation of Sexual Intercourse," *Journal of Marriage and the Family* (1997).